AFFORDABLE JUSTICE

how to settle any dispute, including divorce, out of court

Elizabeth L. Allen, J.D.   **Donald D. Mohr, M.A.**

West Coast Press

E JUSTICE

how to settle any dispute, including divorce, out of court

Elizabeth L. Allen, J.D. and Donald D. Mohr, M.A.

Published by: West Coast Press
4401 Manchester Avenue, Ste. 202
Encinitas, CA 92024
800-494-9866

Copyright © 1997
by Elizabeth L. Allen and Donald D. Mohr
First Printing 1997. Printed in the U. S. of America

Publisher's Cataloging in Publication
(Prepared by Quality Books Inc.)

Allen, Elizabeth L.
    Affordable justice: how to settle any dispute, including divorce, out of court / Elizabeth L. Allen, Donald D. Mohr.
        p.cm.
        ISBN 0-9655876-7-3

1. Conflict management. 2. Divorce mediation. 3. Mediation.
I. Mohr, Donald D. II. Title

HM136.A55 1997   303.6'9

ABOUT THIS BOOK

Introduction

What's wrong with the way we handle disputes? *Something* must be wrong, because millions of people are dissatisfied with our current system. Fortunately, affordable justice is available. The Introduction gives you a quick overview of how to get it and lists the kinds of disputes that can best be resolved out of court.

SECTION 1

Mediation: A User's Guide

A shift from fighting it out in court to figuring it out in mediation is under way. Although trained mediators are readily available, many people are still unaware that mediation provides a quick, inexpensive way to resolve disputes. This section explains how mediation works and how you can use it to your advantage.

SECTION 2

Divorce: Avoiding the Horrors of Court

Contrary to popular opinion, a divorce doesn't have to devastate you financially or emotionally. In divorce mediation, *you* control what happens. You are in charge of how long the process takes and of the outcome. This section explains how you and your family can get through a divorce with dignity, at a price you can afford.

Section 3

When Things Go Sour in the Workplace

If you own a business, you know that disputes are inevitable. Problems with a partner, an employee, a client, or a customer can arise when you least expect them. If you work for someone else, you may face a dispute with a co-worker, or even your boss. This section provides information about how to handle the minor set-backs, as well as the major blow-ups, that occur in the workplace.

Section 4

Dealing with Life's Other Catastrophes

If you are like most people, you are faced with your share of disputes. Things that should go smoothly can go wrong. Simple things like buying a home, renting an apartment, or driving a car can lead to disputes that end up as lawsuits. This section explains how to resolve everyday problems more easily, using mediation and arbitration, instead of resorting to the courts for relief.

Section 5

Negotiating Your Best Deal

Understanding and being able to use effective negotiating techniques can enhance your chances of success in a mediation. This section gives you the tools that you need to achieve the best results in all of your negotiations.

SECTION 6

Choosing the Right Mediator for the Job

Mediators fall into three distinctly different groups. The chances are that one will suit your needs better than the others. This section describes the differences between mediators, so that you can make an informed choice.

SECTION 7

Arbitration: A User's Guide

Choosing an arbitrator is like choosing a judge. You need a person who is competent to evaluate the evidence you present and has the time to give your case the special attention that it deserves. This section explains how to use arbitration to get swift justice when mediation doesn't work.

Directory of Referral Sources And Providers

The Directory is conveniently divided into three parts. The first lists organizations which can refer you to mediators and arbitrators in your area, the second lists providers that maintain offices in a number of locations, and the third lists individual providers.

TABLE OF CONTENTS

Introduction

SECTION 1

Mediation: A User's Guide

SECTION 2

Divorce: Avoiding the Horrors of Court

SECTION 3

When Things Go Sour in the Workplace

SECTION 4

Dealing with Life's Other Catastrophes

SECTION 5

Negotiating Your Best Deal

SECTION 6

Choosing the Right Mediator for the Job

SECTION 7

Arbitration: A User's Guide

Directory of Referral Sources and Providers

Dedication

To Elizabeth's father, Richard C. Lewis, who always wanted to publish a book of his own, and to Donald's father, J. Paul Mohr, who pursued excellence in his own quiet way.

Acknowledgements

Thanks to all the friends and family who urged us on and believed in us as we walked the long road from concept to completion. Thanks also to the many colleagues who contributed their own stories, and to those who helped us check our information and polish our work. The names of these contributors and reviewers appear on pages 160-163.

INTRODUCTION

Using lawyers and courts to resolve disputes can be expensive, time-consuming, and frustrating. Fortunately, you have two alternatives that are likely to produce more satisfying results. The first step is to understand that most conflicts are resolvable, and that even the most impossible case can usually be settled quickly and inexpensively, out of court. The second step is to become familiar with new and better ways to resolve disputes and to be able to use them when the need arises.

In almost every instance, filing a lawsuit and taking your case to court ought to be your *last* resort, not your first choice. You've got other options that you may not even know exist. For instance, you can use mediation to work out a settlement. Whether millions of dollars are at stake, or the dispute is one that can't be measured in money, the chances are that a mediator can help you and the other side reach a satisfactory settlement. The resulting agreement will be legally binding and fully enforceable by a court.

Mediation can work, whether you are involved in a divorce, a contract dispute, an automobile accident claim, or any other type of case that would normally be handled in court. Not surprisingly, mediation does not work 100% of the time. If it fails to produce a settlement, you can move on to binding arbitration, which gives you a second chance to arrive at a cost-effective, speedy resolution to your problem. In most cases, you can opt either to handle the mediation or the arbitration by yourself or to hire an attorney to assist you; the choice is yours.

When Can You Use Mediation or Arbitration?

divorces
post-divorce modifications
prenuptial agreements
dissolution of non-marital relationships
contract disputes
real estate disputes
insurance claims
victim-offender issues
school site conflicts
partnership dissolutions
neighborhood disputes
labor-management disputes
sexual harassment claims
employment termination issues
construction defect claims
product liability claims
adoption planning
estate distribution disputes

Section 1
MEDIATION: A USER'S GUIDE

One:
Mediation--The New Hope

- We've had a wake-up call! It's time to stop relying on the old legal system to solve our problems, large and small, and to start using mediation to achieve justice *more affordably.*

- Every couple contemplating divorce should know that mediation is an option that is likely to reduce the wear and tear on themselves and their children.

- Every business person should be aware that dollars can be added to the bottom line, by using mediation in any dispute where direct negotiation has failed.

- Every employer should realize that using mediation to resolve a problem with an employee can result not only in enormous financial savings, but also in improved morale and productivity.

- Every employee should understand that the fastest way to resolve a dispute that originated in the workplace is to settle it through mediation.

- Each homeowner, renter, and landlord should take advantage of the hundreds of dispute resolution centers that offer free or inexpensive assistance in resolving problems with neighbors, landlords, and tenants.

*"The notion that most people
want black-robed judges,
well-dressed lawyers
and fine-paneled courtrooms
as the setting to resolve
their disputes is not correct.
People with problems,
like people with pains,
want relief, and they want it
as quickly and inexpensively as
possible."*

Warren E. Burger, Chief Justice
United States Supreme Court

Two:
How It Works

- A mediator, or a team of mediators, meets with two or more people who are having a dispute to help them negotiate a settlement.

- Mediation sessions are usually held in the mediator's office; however, they can take place in almost any setting, including a business office, a school, a church, or a condominium clubhouse.

- Once all of the participants are assembled, the mediator describes his or her role, as well as the role of the participants. Then everyone signs a mediation agreement, which describes the mediation process, lists the ground rules, and states the mediator's fees. Occasionally, some of the ground rules are negotiated as the first step in the process, before other issues are addressed.

- After the preliminaries have been completed, everyone takes turns stating his or her view of the situation, without interruption. Following the opening remarks, the mediator usually summarizes what each side has said.

- Next, the mediator identifies the issues involved in the dispute and writes them on a board. The participants then indicate to the mediator which issues have been resolved and which have not.

- Once the unresolved issues have been identified, the mediator selects the easiest issue to start on, in order to maximize the possibility of success.

- Everyone involved is invited to propose solutions. If attorneys are present, they join the disputants and the mediators in this search. As the process continues, each option is evaluated, with the disputants selecting those that best meet their needs. This process continues until all issues are resolved.

- Working through a mediation is like putting a puzzle together. First you find a small piece that fits here, then one that fits there, and then gradually the entire picture emerges, piece by piece.

- After all of the issues have been resolved, an agreement is written and signed. Sometimes a handwritten agreement is signed by the participants on the day of the mediation. However, in cases involving large amounts of money or many complex issues, a formal agreement is prepared following the mediation for signing at a later date.

- Most mediators *encourage* each participant to have the agreement reviewed by an attorney prior to signing it. Some mediators *require* the participants to have the proposed agreement reviewed by outside counsel.

- It's not unusual for a mediation to take more than one session. In fact, divorce mediations usually take at least three sessions, and sometimes as many as ten or twelve.

- In cases where the dispute has been filed with the court as a lawsuit prior to mediation, the mediated agreement is submitted to the court as a "stipulated judgment," for the judge to sign too.

Three:
Why It Works

- One of the reasons that mediation works is that the mediator helps the participants understand each other's feelings and beliefs about the dispute.

- Equally important, participants are permitted to tell their stories without interruption; they get what feels like their "day in court."

- The mediation agreement and, in some states, the laws of evidence dictate that statements made in a mediation and documents prepared for the purpose of the mediation are not admissible in court, except by agreement of all involved. Because the mediation process is confidential, people generally feel that they can be more candid than they could if they were facing off for a court battle.

- Mediation works because the dispute is reframed by the mediators into a *cooperative search* for solutions that meet the needs of both parties, not a battle for determination of who was right and who was wrong.

- Mediation works because large, complex issues are broken down into their component parts, and the easiest issues are resolved first.

- Mediation works because most people do not want to stay involved in a dispute any longer than necessary; they want to resolve it and move on.

*"Discourage litigation.
Persuade your neighbors to
compromise whenever you can.
Point out to them how the
nominal winner is often a real loser--
in fees, expenses, and waste of time."*

Abraham Lincoln

Four:
The Mediator's Job

- The mediator must remain neutral and uninvested in the outcome of the mediation.

- The mediator sets and enforces ground rules, insuring that each participant is treated respectfully and that discussions focus on issues, not personalities.

- The mediator guides the participants in discussing and exploring all of the issues, making sure that each participant has had enough time to reach carefully considered decisions.

- The mediator, a trained listener and observer, attends to both verbal and nonverbal language, in order to facilitate better communication among the participants.

- The mediator summarizes statements made by each participant, often *reframing* what a person says, so that the message is less inflammatory and more easily heard by the other side.

- A good mediator helps generate creative options, increasing the number of possible solutions for each issue in the dispute, and encouraging new approaches to problem-solving.

- An inventive mediator identifies and proposes "high-low exchanges," where one side can give something to the other side which is of low value to the person giving it and high value to the recipient.

- The mediator encourages, empathizes with, and reassures the participants, so that they keep a positive outlook and don't give up.

- The mediator helps remove emotional barriers to conflict resolution, by encouraging each participant to express his or her feelings about disputed events and issues. When emotional barriers are removed, the dispute becomes much easier to resolve.

- If and when the participants reach an agreement, the mediator writes either a formal *settlement agreement* or a less formal *memorandum of understanding* ("MOU").

- In some types of mediation, such as divorce mediation, the mediator may provide legal and tax information to the participants, prepare all of the required court documents, and draft auxiliary documents, such as deeds.

The Mediator's Job

To empower disputing parties, by assisting them in the exercise of self-determination to decide whether and how to resolve their dispute.

To promote mutual recognition between disputing parties, by providing a nonadversarial opportunity to air their differences and realize each other's common humanity.

Robert A. Baruch Bush, Professor of Law

Five:
Your Job

- **Organize.** Organize your thoughts about the dispute, so that you can clearly express your view of what happened and propose solutions.

- **Come prepared.** Arrive at the mediation prepared, with all of your facts and figures in writing. Bring copies of important documents for everyone. If reports and written opinions are relevant, bring them too. What you can show in writing from objective sources will add credibility to your position.

- **Listen.** During the mediation, everyone listens to the others in the group give their version of the situation. If you listen carefully to each person, rather than formulating your rebuttal, your chances of succeeding in mediation are increased. Instead of interrupting, make a note when someone says something that you want to respond to later.

- **Learn.** In all likelihood, your past efforts at communicating with the other side were unsuccessful. Pay attention when the mediator suggests different ways of communicating. These new tools will improve your chances of hearing the other side and of being heard by them.

- **Be careful.** If you find that you need more information in order to make an informed decision, take the time to get it. Then get any outside help you may need in order to analyze the information. Weigh each decision in light of the whole picture, keeping each agreement you make tentative, until the entire agreement takes shape.

- *Be realistic.* Don't cling to a fantasy about your chances of winning in court. Remember that although you could receive a windfall, you might also lose. Win or lose, you will pay a price to take your case to trial. Before the mediation, obtain informed, objective opinions from attorneys about both the strong *and* the weak points in your case.

- *Negotiate in good faith.* Don't waste everyone's time by going through mediation, if you do not wish to settle your case. If you have been ordered into mediation by a judge and have no intention of settling out of court, make your position clear at the outset.

- *Sit tight.* Every mediation has its difficult moments. A good mediator will help get you past what may *appear* to be an impasse. Stay with the process and give everyone involved another chance to reach a successful conclusion. The odds are that your case *will* settle.

---

*Three-fourths of the miseries
and misunderstandings in
the world will disappear if we step
into the shoes of our adversaries
and understand their viewpoint.*

Gandhi

Six:
The Cast of Characters

- In the traditional legal system, lawyers often appear in court in place of the parties. In mediation, the individuals involved in the dispute are expected to be present and to participate. Each person who is part of the problem, or whose consent is important in reaching a solution, should be required to attend; otherwise, the participants are probably wasting their time.

- For example, when two couples are arguing over the location of their common fence, all four people should participate in the mediation, even though one or two of them may have remained in the background. If a person who is involved, even indirectly, in the dispute fails to attend the mediation, he or she may later sabotage the agreement.

- In the case of a two-car collision, both drivers should participate in the mediation. Only they can apologize, and an apology can be worth thousands of dollars. The insurance adjuster controls the purse strings and needs to attend too, in order to negotiate the financial aspects of the settlement.

- When a couple goes through a post-divorce mediation over changing the parenting plan, the stepparents, the grandparents, and the children themselves may all play active roles.

- In addition to the disputants, the cast of characters in a mediation includes one or more mediators, and may include one or more attorneys.

"*You have a pretty good case, Mr. Pitkin.
How much justice can you afford?*"

Seven:
Attorneys--An Optional *Feature*

- No one knows your dispute like you do. Unless your situation is extremely complicated, or you feel overwhelmed by the details or by your own emotions, you can handle the mediation sessions without an attorney.

- Another option is to employ an attorney as a legal *consultant.* You can get information and advice from him or her before the mediation begins, between sessions, and/or before you sign the final agreement.

- When finances are limited, people usually choose either *not* to have an attorney, or to ask an attorney to be "on call" to give advice over the phone during the mediation.

- If you decide to use an attorney, remember that the terms of the settlement are still in your hands. You, not your attorney, will have to live with the results.

- If the other side brings an attorney to the mediation, you may want to bring along an advocate too, in order to keep things balanced.

- Many divorce mediators do not permit attorneys to attend the mediation sessions. This is a wise policy, since divorces are resolved more easily when only the husband and wife participate. If your mediator excludes attorneys, you can still consult with one ahead of time and/or between sessions, if you choose.

*"The more a person knows
about the legal profession
and the more he or she is in
direct personal contact with lawyers,
the lower an individual's
opinion of them."*

American Bar Association Journal Survey

Eight:
It's Safe

- Mediation is safe, because you're not locked in. You can always go to court, if the other side doesn't negotiate in good faith, or if for any other reason you don't reach an agreement that you can live with.

- It's safe, because you sign a settlement agreement only if you believe that it will work for you.

- It's safe, because you can get all of the information that you need to make decisions about each issue, before you sign a final agreement.

- It's safe, because you can get any outside legal advice that you may want, before or during the mediation.

- It's safe, because the mediator will not allow anyone to be abusive, threatening, or belittling.

- It's safe, because it doesn't matter how hard the other side tries to influence the mediator, the mediator won't make the decisions, you will.

- It's safe, because you can take a break at any time, resuming mediation only when you are ready to continue.

- It's safe, because when the agreement involves a promise to do something, other than to make a final payment, you can test it out during a trial period. If the plan is successful, sign the agreement. If not, return to mediation to fine-tune it, until you are satisfied that it meets your needs.

What Makes Mediation Different?

	Negotiation	Mediation	Arbitration	Litigation
Control of the process	Parties control directly	Parties share control with the mediator	Arbitrator and attorneys control	Judge and attorneys control
Parties' control of the outcome	Complete	Complete (unless a judge's signature is required)	None	None
Cost to parties	$	$$	$$$	$$$$$$
Legal effect	Binding; modifiable if both sides agree to a change	Binding; modifiable if both sides agree to a change	Binding or nonbinding, by agreement ahead of time	Binding, but appealable to a higher court

Nine:
It's Legal

- People often ask whether an agreement that results from a mediation is *legally binding*. The answer is "**yes**."

- If you have any reason to doubt whether your mediated agreement will be considered legally binding by a court, have it reviewed by an attorney *before* you sign it.

- If your mediation ends *without* an agreement, you will not be bound by anything. At that point you are free to drop the matter entirely or to pursue other options. These options include: direct negotiation with the other side, negotiation through attorneys, arbitration, or trial. You are, in most respects, "back to square one."

- Certain people don't meet the legal requirements to enter into a binding contract, including a mediated settlement agreement. Minors and those with significant mental impairments are deemed lacking in the capacity to make a valid contract. Generally, an agreement that they sign is unenforceable in court.

- A mediated settlement agreement is a binding contract, enforceable in court. Furthermore, if it is made part of a court order following the mediation, anyone failing to comply with it can be held in contempt of court.

*"For the most part,
we depend upon judicial processes
to settle our grievances.
Perhaps we've even created
the clumsy strictures of the courts
to keep our savageries in check.
The problem is
that so often the law
seems pale in its remedies,
leaving us restless and unfulfilled
in our craving for satisfaction."*

Sue Grafton, "K" is for Killer

Ten:
You Get Your "Day in Court"

- In order to feel as though justice has been done, you need to have your "day in court," an opportunity to tell your side of the story and to be heard. If your case is handled in court, you're not likely to be allowed to do this. Generally, you are permitted only to respond to a lawyer's questions. You may not be able to testify at all, except through written *declarations*. Matters of importance to you may be deemed *irrelevant* by the court.

- In mediation, you'll have numerous opportunities to say what you want to say, without interruption. You can tell your story in a narrative version, rather than merely responding to questions.

- You'll be free to state the facts as you view them, whether or not they fit within the court's definition of legally admissible evidence.

- You'll have a chance to talk about the anger, hurt, and frustration that you may have experienced as a result of the dispute.

- You'll be able to ask questions and to propose solutions that meet your specific needs.

- You'll have the satisfaction of knowing that you've been heard by the mediators and by the other side.

- By telling the story yourself, you can be sure to tell it exactly the way that you see it, without the errors and omissions that can occur when you hire someone to do your talking for you.

*"Justice is an insignificant
concept in today's legal system.
Attorneys who specialize in civil
litigation--the personal injury cases,
contract disputes, malpractice cases,
that are the bread and butter
of most practices--are simply
more interested in winning cases
than in solving disputes
by finding a fair solution.*

*When people pay an attorney
$250 an hour,
they do not want compromise;
they want their attorney
to do battle with all guns blazing.
The theory is that with the two sides
battling it out tooth and nail,
the deserving party will prevail.
The reality is that the side that strikes
hardest and fastest is often
likely to prevail, regardless of
the relative merits of their cases."*

Sam Benson, Attorney at Law

Eleven:
Information is Power

- The more you know about the details of your dispute, the better your chances of resolving it successfully in mediation.

- If you need expert help in order to understand some technical aspect of your case, you can get it. For example, you might need information from a lawyer, an accountant, a real estate appraiser, or a contractor, in order to evaluate data that either you or the other side has brought to the table.

- You can request that an outside expert summarize information, offer an opinion, write a report, or consult with another expert on your behalf.

- You may want to get advice about your legal rights. Many mediators will provide you with basic legal *information*; however, if you need legal *advice*, you should see an outside attorney. Even if your mediator is also an attorney, he or she cannot provide you with legal *advice*, since to do so would compromise the mediator's role, which is to remain neutral.

- In a traditional lawsuit, both sides hire their own experts on each disputed issue, at great expense. In mediation, people often agree to use a single expert to provide the information that both sides need, such as an appraisal of value or an estimate of the cost of repair. The decision to cooperate in the hiring of experts that are acceptable to both sides can save thousands of dollars.

A Builder's Nightmare

The trouble started during the first rainfall after the office building was purchased. The glass wall which formed the exterior of the building had leaked, causing major damage to the interior. The owner sued both the developer and the contractor, claiming that the wall needed to be torn down and replaced, at a cost of $750,000. The defendants insisted that the joints could be resealed, at a cost of only $100,000.

A mediation session was held, but both sides stuck to their guns. Then the mediator scheduled a separate session, to which only the construction experts were invited. Working together, the experts were able to agree on repair specifications, which involved replacement of a portion of the window system and resealing of the rest of the joints, at a cost of $160,000. Both sides accepted the plan and settled out of court shortly thereafter.

Michael J. Roberts, Attorney and Mediator

Twelve:
You Decide What's Fair

- Obtaining justice means getting a fair result. If you take your case to trial, a judge or jury will decide your fate. If you submit your case to arbitration, an arbitrator will determine the outcome. Even though you are certain that the law is on your side, the judge, jury, or arbitrator may rule against you, for reasons that may never be clear to you.

- In a mediation, *you* make the decisions. In most cases, you and the other side are free to ignore the law entirely and base your decisions on your own personal sense of fairness instead.

- Although it makes sense to know your legal rights, most people want to use their *own* sense of fairness as the standard for resolving a dispute. In mediation the controlling question is, "What outcome will *both sides* consider the best way to meet their needs?"

- People who go through a trial often feel that they weren't treated fairly. They blame the law, the judge, or their attorney when things don't go the way they want them to.

- Mediation is different. You are in control. You are the decision-maker and the judge of what is or isn't fair. You have the comfort of knowing that if a proposed agreement doesn't seem fair to you, you don't have to sign it. In mediation, unlike in court, the outcome doesn't hold any *surprises*.

*"The entire legal profession,
lawyers, judges,
law school teachers,
has become so mesmerized with the
stimulation of the courtroom contest
that we tend to forget that
we should be healers of conflicts.*

*For some disputes,
trials will be the only means,
but for many claims. . .
our system is too costly, too painful,
too destructive, too inefficient
for a truly civilized people.
To rely on the adversarial process
as the principal means
of resolving conflicting claims
is a mistake that must be corrected."*

Chief Justice Warren E. Burger

Thirteen:
You Create a Custom Plan

- In mediation you can help create an agreement that meets your own unique needs, one that works for you. You can avoid having a cookie-cutter plan imposed upon you by a court that has only limited time to consider your particular situation. In mediation, with few exceptions, you are free to enter into any agreement that both sides can live with.

- You can include in your agreement minute *details* regarding each side's rights and responsibilities.

- Your plan can be more *creative* than anything that a judge could or would order. It might include payment in goods or services, instead of cash. It might also include items whose monetary value is difficult to determine, such as a letter of recommendation from an employer or an agreement to repair a dangerous condition.

- In mediation, you can propose any solution or make any agreement that suits you. In certain instances, such as disputes involving child support or payment of damages to a minor, the judge has the final word. In these cases, you must submit the settlement agreement to the court for approval, in order for it to become legally binding.

- Whenever possible, you should create an agreement that not only resolves the current dispute, but also outlines the steps to follow if, and when, disputes arise in the future.

The Case of the Greasy Dumpster

Bill slipped on some grease which was leaking from a dumpster behind a row of restaurants, injuring himself in the fall. He sued the mall and the restaurant owners, and then decided to attempt an out-of-court settlement through mediation. Had the case gone to court, questions of whose grease might have been in the puddle, how much responsibility Bill bore by walking in the alley, and who was responsible for maintenance around the dumpster would have cost time and money to answer.

Instead, the mediation focused on finding solutions, rather than on fixing blame. The owners saw that Bill was not a vagrant, but rather a respectable person out on a lunch break. Bill's injury was acknowledged by one of the defense attorneys, who had suffered a similar one. Bill saw that the restaurant owners were not the unfeeling people that he had pictured. Through discussion, both sides got what they needed emotionally and were then able to reach a financial settlement. Bill settled for half the money that he had demanded, which was more than enough to cover his medical expenses. One restaurant owner that couldn't afford to pay, gave Bill coupons for free meals.

Betty McManus, Mediator

Fourteen:
You Control the Outcome

- In mediation, you have *maximum* control over the outcome; in court, you have *minimum* control. In mediation, *you,* not a judge, an arbitrator, an attorney, or a mediator, have the power to decide your future. In a few specific instances, such as cases involving minors, a judge's approval is required. Most of the time, however, you and the other side are free to fashion any agreement that suits you.

- If you can't resolve *all* of the issues in your dispute by means of mediation, you may be able to settle *most* of them. By doing so, you maintain control over the parts of the dispute that you *can* settle, leaving only the parts that you can't resolve to someone else to decide.

- Many people have been convinced that they had a slam dunk of a lawsuit, only to discover later that the judge or jury saw things differently. By reaching an agreement through mediation, you foreclose the possibility of a surprise verdict against you.

- In mediation, you can use your powers of persuasion to reach your goals. Even when the law is not technically on your side, you may be able to convince the other side to see things your way. You are not restricted by the law.

- In mediation, you wield *all* of the power. Unless a proposed settlement agreement meets with *your* approval, you will not sign it. *That's* power.

"Mediation's attraction stems from the public's phenomenal dissatisfaction with the court system. The feeling is that there is no justice in the courts and that people can solve their problems better themselves. They are looking for something different, and mediation provides that."

Judith Filner, Attorney at Law
National Institute for Dispute Resolution

Fifteen:
You Can Start Anytime

- One of the advantages of mediation is that you can resolve your dispute on *your* schedule. You don't have to wait for an attorney to prepare your case or for a judge to be available to hear it.

- You don't even have to file a lawsuit. As soon as you are faced with a problem that you can't resolve yourself, contact a mediator and set up an appointment. Some mediators are willing to call the other side and encourage them to participate; others will ask you to contact the other side.

- If you or your opponent has already filed a lawsuit, it's not too late to mediate. Contact the other side and ask them to postpone the court action while you try mediation. If they agree, your court hearing can be postponed until a later date. Courts are generally willing to grant a continuance, if the parties decide to mediate. If the mediation is not successful, you can still have an arbitrator or a judge decide your case at a later time.

- Rarely do disputes improve with age. When you are ready to work out a solution with the other side, you are better off if you can get going without delay. If both sides agree, you can usually schedule the mediation to start within a week or so.

- The more money you have invested in winning your lawsuit, the harder it may be to give up the adversarial process and work on a settlement. Mediation is generally best used as an *early* intervention.

PEANUTS reprinted by permission of United Feature Syndicate, Inc.

Sixteen:
It's a Real Time-Saver

- If everyone involved in a dispute wants to resolve it and move on, mediation can save years.

- You won't have to spend time preparing for trial. You won't have to: attend depositions (sworn pre-trial testimony), answer the other side's interrogatories (written testimony under oath), or comply with the other side's subpenas (requests for records). You won't have to deal with the delay of appealing a decision that you can't live with.

- A comparison of similar cases reveals that mediation usually takes only a fraction of the time that litigation takes.

- Even multimillion dollar lawsuits can often be settled in a couple of mediation sessions. The same case handled within the traditional court system might take several *years*, unless the court has established a "fast-track" system to speed up the process. Even then, the courts have to put criminal cases ahead of civil cases, so your lawsuit may proceed at a snail's pace.

- Every day that your dispute remains unresolved is a day when your time, energy, and money could be directed toward other, more pleasant and productive, pursuits. If you resolve your dispute in *two days* through mediation, instead of *two years* through litigation, you've saved 728 days.

- In a mediation involving many different issues, such as a divorce mediation, *several* sessions may be required to reach a final agreement. Even so, you will probably finish much sooner than you would have, had you engaged in a court battle.

- You and the other participants in a mediation determine the length of each session, as well as the number of days or weeks between sessions. Most people experience a decrease in their ability to focus and negotiate effectively after three or four hours, even with occasional breaks. Adjourning the mediation until another day is better than continuing when everyone is tired.

- Some mediators recommend marathon sessions, where meals are brought in and negotiations continue until a settlement is finally reached. So long as all participants feel that they can think clearly, lengthy sessions can be useful, especially when people have traveled a great distance and are eager to reach a settlement before returning home. Warning: Don't let anyone pressure you into continuing a session past the point where you are focusing clearly on your best interests.

- The primary factor in determining the time needed to complete an entire mediation is the *readiness* of each of the participants to reach resolution. Just as a chain is only as strong as its weakest link, a mediation can proceed only as fast as the most reluctant participant will allow. If one person holds out for the "principal of the matter," the entire mediation can be stalled, or even derailed.

Seventeen:
It's Cheaper

- Lawsuits are risky ventures. Many people have learned the hard way that you can throw good money after bad pursuing justice in court.

- Because our legal system is so complicated, and doesn't include steps that foster early settlement, the fee that you have to pay to a lawyer to handle even a simple case is usually measured in thousands of dollars. That expenditure doesn't always make sense, especially in a situation where your attorney's fees may equal or exceed your potential winnings.

- Non-profit dispute resolution centers, which are funded through tax dollars, private donations, and court filing fees, are located throughout the United States. The volunteer mediators who staff these centers handle a wide range of disputes. They are perfectly suited to handling the case of the barking dog, the noisy neighbor, and the troublesome teenager. If your case involves a great deal of money and you decide to use a community dispute resolution center, make sure that the coordinator assigns you to the center's top mediators.

- On the other hand, when the financial stakes are high, your best choice may be to use a *private* mediator. Even if you retain an attorney to help with your mediation, your overall cost, including attorney's fees, will be modest, relative to what you would pay if you took your case to court.

- In mediation, you can save on other costs too. You won't need to pay experts to testify at trial. You won't need to pay jury fees. You won't miss much time from work. You won't have to pay for the appeal which could result, if you or the other side is dissatisfied with the court's verdict.

- After a trial, the winner often has to *make* the other side pay. All too often, the loser files bankruptcy or hides assets and gets away without paying at all. Unfortunately, many people who win at trial never actually receive a single dollar.

- When people successfully go through a mediation, they generally comply with their settlement agreement. This means that if the other side agrees to pay, the chances are extremely high that they will actually do so. If necessary, as with any other contract that is breached, you can use the court to enforce the agreement.

More than 4,000 companies have signed the Center for Public Resources Corporate Policy Statement on Alternatives to Litigation. In the five-year period ending in 1995, 652 of the companies reported legal cost savings totaling more than $200 million, with an average savings of more than $300,000 per company.

Center for Public Resources
Institute for Dispute Resolution

Eighteen:
It Gets the Job Done

- The majority of cases that are handled through mediation end up with an agreement. Although no one can *guarantee* that your case will settle, the odds are heavily in your favor.

- When people go through mediation, they usually iron out all of the issues that they have with the other side. They take the time to work through and finish whatever problems exist between them.

- Because most mediators encourage the participants to express their feelings about the disputed issues, people generally feel better after the mediation is concluded.

- By contrast, after a trial, people often feel angrier than they did when the dispute began. They seldom feel that they were heard or got their day in court. Because they don't feel that justice was done, they return to court time and again. This happens frequently after people are divorced. They return to court repeatedly to fight over the kids, because they never really finished their fight when they were going through their divorce. They remain connected in the only way they know--through their ongoing court battle.

- Mediation is most likely to succeed when both sides realize that each has something to gain by participating in the mediation and something to lose by going to court. The process works even when people are initially doubtful about the possibility of reaching a settlement.

The U.S. Army Corps of Engineers Alternative Dispute Resolution (ADR) and Partnering Program has made significant strides in reversing an overwhelming trend of litigation. This program has prevented litigation in several hundred major contracts, reducing expected annual claims liability by hundreds of millions of dollars. Hazardous and/or toxic waste cleanup has accelerated on several sites. Long-festering conflicts over operation of some large, multi-purpose dams have been resolved in months, rather than years.

U.S. Army Corps of Engineers
Office of the Chief Counsel

Nineteen:
It's Private

- Most of us don't want our disputes aired in public. Nonetheless, cases handled in court are generally presented in front of anyone who happens or chooses to be there, providing grist for the rumor mill. To protect the participants' privacy, mediations are usually held in an office, where only those directly involved are privy to the discussion.

- At the beginning of a mediation, everyone present signs a Mediation Agreement, which includes a statement about confidentiality. Each participant agrees not to use statements made during the mediation or documents prepared for the purpose of the mediation as evidence in court. The Agreement also prevents the participants from successfully subpenaing the mediator, or his or her records, into court, except in the case of a criminal offense.

- In order to keep outsiders, including the media, from finding out what transpires in a mediation, the Mediation Agreement can be drafted with further restrictions against divulging anything to outsiders, including family and friends. This additional safeguard ensures *maximum* privacy.

- Some states make mediations confidential by statute. Although these laws vary in their scope, they generally preclude the admission into evidence of statements made during the mediation or documents prepared for the purpose of the mediation.

The Navajo Peacemaker Court System

The Navajos have a conflict resolution process that they used in ancient times, known as the "peacemaker court system." It is based upon their concept of conflict resolution, which is to restore harmony. They believe that if one ends a dispute by having a winner and a loser, one dispute may have ended, but another dispute surely will have started, because harmony will not have been restored. They believe that coercion is not an effective way to bring about genuine change in any individual's long-term behavior or attitude. Coercion is a short-term, not a long-term, answer.

Judge Anne Kass
Second Judicial District
Albuquerque, New Mexico

Twenty:
Healing--Part of the Process

- When disputes are handled in court, healing rarely occurs. Our legal system fosters acrimony, hostility, separateness, and blame, not reconciliation and forgiveness.

- Opposing attorneys often instruct their clients not to communicate with each other. This practice effectively forestalls not only the resolution of the conflict, but also healing.

- In mediation, healing is possible. As the process begins, each person listens to the other's views. As it progresses, each participant is encouraged by the mediator to walk in the shoes of the person on the other side of the table. Understanding the other person's feelings and the motivation behind his or her actions promotes healing. When healing occurs, disputants can put the past behind them and move on. In a completely successful mediation, forgiveness takes place; sometimes it occurs even if the dispute is not totally resolved.

- When maintaining an ongoing relationship with the other side is desirable, damage repair is especially important. Parents do their children a favor by healing the wounds that are inflicted during a divorce. People involved in a business dispute can also benefit by repairing the damage to their relationship. During the mediation process, each side has the opportunity to forgive the other and to bury the hatchet.

Sewer Construction Run Amok

The cost of defending a lawsuit, even one without any basis in fact, can be devastating to the bottom-line for any company. Our firm experienced this when a contract to design a city sewer system went sour. The city that hired us fired the first contractor for shoddy workmanship. Then the contractor sued the city, contending that his work had met all of the specifications.

Concerned that the city might lose the lawsuit and then turn around and sue us, our company assisted in the city's legal defense, paying over $500,000 to defense attorneys and spending $100,000 of our own engineering funds. After more than three years of litigation, in order to dispose of the case, the city settled with the contractor, who accepted a small fraction of the amount that he had originally demanded. When it was all over, the damage to our company was two-fold: our legal costs exceeded our profit, and we won't get any more work from that city, because of the negative stories that ran in the local media and the bad taste the entire incident left in everybody's mouth.

Twenty-Two:
Focus on the Future, not the Past

- In our traditional legal system, we delve into the past, searching for evidence to prove that the other side was at fault. We identify the wrongdoer and order him or her to repay the injured party. This system works better in theory than in practice.

- As a participant in a mediation, you will focus on finding solutions, not on fixing blame. You and the others will engage in a cooperative search for ways to resolve the problems of the past and to move on.

- At the beginning of the mediation, you will have ample opportunity to tell your story in detail. Once you have done so, and believe that your views and feelings have been heard, you will be more able to concentrate on finding solutions, instead of rehashing old issues and injuries.

- Focusing on the future means giving everyone a chance to start afresh, relating to each other in a more positive way than they did in the past.

- If you believe that the other side will not live up to their agreements, raise your concerns during the mediation. Bring up your fears about what could go wrong, and suggest ways to ensure the other side's compliance. Build safeguards into the agreement which are designed to maximize its chances of being carried out.

A Ploy that Backfired

The board of directors of a condo association hired a contractor (later my client) to repair the decking in their 12-unit complex. When the work was done, they refused to make the final payment of $6,000, so after attempting unsuccessfully to reach a settlement, we filed a lawsuit to collect the balance due. The association then filed a counterclaim for $25,000, alleging, among other things, that my client had botched the job by using the wrong coating on the decks.

The board's counterclaim forced us to hire a construction defect expert, take depositions, and go through an 8-day jury trial, which we won. When the association refused to pay the judgment, which included the original $6,000, plus $22,000 for my attorney's fees, the court ordered the association to pay the monthly homeowners' dues to my client. Instead of doing so, the board assessed each owner $2,500, forcing these innocent individuals to bear the consequences of the board's refusal to pay a legitimate bill.

A. David Puzo, Attorney

Twenty-Three:
Managing Future Disputes

- When you know that you'll have to co-exist with another person or business in the future, it's useful to have a plan for how to handle the disputes that may arise. Some problems cannot be avoided, but can be dealt with more effectively when they occur if a conflict management plan is in effect.

- Many mediated agreements describe the steps that the parties will take in the event of a future dispute. Creating a system for managing future disputes re-assures those involved in the current one that they will have a set of clearly defined procedures to follow, if trouble arises again. This positive focus makes future disputes, as well as the current dispute, easier to resolve.

Conflict Resolution Steps

1) Each side communicates with the other side directly, attempting to resolve the problem by negotiation.

2) If direct negotiations don't work, both sides enter into mediation, in an attempt to find a cooperative solution, with the assistance of a mediator.

3) If mediation doesn't work, both sides enter into binding arbitration, in order to bring an end to the dispute, without resorting to lengthy, expensive litigation.

A Back Yard Battle

Two couples who owned adjacent homes had fought with each other for years about everything from overhanging trees to over-watered lawns. Finally, one husband tried to run the other husband over with his car. The couples sued and counter-sued each other, returning time and again to court, until a judge eventually referred them to mediation. After two tempestuous sessions, both couples were able to agree on several steps that each would take to remedy past wrongs. More importantly, they included in their agreement a series of steps to follow, if and when problems arose in the future:

1)   They would refrain from bringing up past difficulties and would attempt to work things out among themselves, to the best of their abilities, before seeking outside assistance.

2)   Each couple would discuss the situation between themselves.

3)   If the situation warranted, they would approach the other couple, or one member of the other couple, and discuss the situation.

4)   If the situation was not resolved through informal means, both couples would return to mediation to resolve their differences.

5)   Only in the event that they failed to resolve any future difficulties through mediation would they go back to court.

Twenty-Four:
There's More Than One Way to Do It

- Teachers don't teach alike, judges don't judge alike, and not surprisingly, mediators don't mediate alike. Mediators use a *variety* of approaches, and can be divided into three general categories or groups.

- One school of thought holds that a mediator should do almost *anything* to obtain a settlement, including applying strong pressure. Sometimes this pressure takes the form of a dire prediction about what will happen if the case goes to trial, instead of settling. Retired judges often follow this model. Their opinion carries weight with the participants, because they have had years of experience on the bench. We refer to these mediators as **"muscle mediators."** People who participate in this type of mediation often feel later that they were pressured into an agreement, without adequate time to weigh and consider their options.

- At the other end of the spectrum, some mediators believe that they should *never* offer their own views or give information about the law during a mediation. They function strictly as *facilitators,* offering no opinion about how the participants might fare in court. Mediators in community dispute resolution centers usually follow this model. We refer to these mediators as **"purists."**

- Mediators who follow a third model refrain from pressuring the participants into a hasty settlement; they work more slowly toward resolution. Unlike the purists, however, they offer legal *information* when they think it will be helpful. Sometimes, they give the participants written copies of the laws that relate to their dispute. They may offer an opinion about whether the options under consideration are likely to be accepted by the local courts, but rarely share their own views of what the outcome of the dispute should be. We call this group of mediators the "**centrists**."

- No one model is right for everyone. Whichever model you prefer, consider using a *team* of mediators. Often a team of mediators, can provide the most effective help.

In 1994, 19,004,662 civil law suits were filed in the United States, excluding juvenile offenses, traffic offenses, and federal cases.

American Bar Association

Twenty-Five:
When It Doesn't Work

- Mediation is not likely to be successful when one person is convinced that the other side acted with malice during the disputed incident and is unwilling to reexamine that belief.

- Mediation will rarely succeed when one side is unwilling to make *any* offer to settle the case.

- The chance for a successful mediation is diminished if the parties have been required, by a court for instance, to participate in the mediation.

- Mediation won't work if either party isn't negotiating in good faith.

- The phrase, "That's non-negotiable," is a death knell for a mediation, because it curtails discussion.

- Sometimes mediation doesn't work because one person wants to control everyone and everything and is unwilling to negotiate. That person usually fails to see that if the mediation does not succeed, he or she will have far less control in court, where *all* of the decisions will be made by a judge or jury.

- Mediation won't work if either party is determined to get revenge.

- Mediation won't work if one side is too weak to negotiate and can't be empowered during the mediation process to speak up for their own interests.

- Mediation is not likely to work if either party believes that the mediator is biased in favor of the other side.

- Mediation is unlikely to work if the mediator is not sufficiently skilled to move the parties out of an adversarial stance and involve them in a search for solutions.

- Mediation won't work if the participants get discouraged or frustrated and give up too easily. Reaching an agreement can be long, hard, emotionally exhausting work, but it's always well worth the effort, considering the alternatives. If you're in a mediation and the going gets tough, hang in there and *keep on negotiating*. A skillful mediator can help you pull through, if you're willing to continue the dialogue.

"The law isn't justice.
It's a very imperfect mechanism.
If you press exactly the right buttons
and are also lucky,
justice may show up in the answer.
A mechanism is all the law
was ever intended to be."

Raymond Chandler

Twenty-Six:
When It's Not Appropriate

- Mediation is not appropriate when any participant is mentally, emotionally, or physically unable to negotiate.

- Mediation is not appropriate when one person is so intimidated by the other that he or she is afraid to speak up.

- Mediation is not appropriate when one person is afraid of physical abuse from the other and fears the consequences of telling the truth or making demands.

- Mediation is not appropriate when one party is so out of control emotionally that he or she is unable to focus on the issues under discussion.

- Mediation is not appropriate when one person threatens another during the process. All participants need to feel free to state their needs, without fear of reprisal.

- Mediation is not appropriate when someone who was part of the problem refuses to participate. An axiom of mediation is that everyone who was part of the problem, or could play a part in the solution, should participate in the mediation.

- Mediation is not appropriate when one or more of the participants is under the influence of a mind-altering drug or alcohol.

Section 2 -- *DIVORCE: AVOIDING THE HORRORS OF COURT*

Twenty-Seven:
Designing Your Own Agreement

- When you mediate the terms of your divorce, you design your own agreement, with the mediator's assistance.

- At the beginning of the process, the mediator will make a list, with your help, of all the issues to be discussed. These usually include spousal support, child support, the payment of debts, the division of assets, and a parenting plan.

- You may have made decisions about one or more of the issues in your divorce prior to beginning mediation. However, most mediators consider each agreement to be *tentative* until *all* decisions have been made. Keeping agreements tentative gives you the freedom to revise them as you get more information and see the entire picture unfold.

- As you become aware of the number and complexity of the decisions to be made, the task may seem overwhelming. Part of your mediator's job is to guide you through the process by isolating the issues, so that you and your spouse can deal with them one at a time.

- In order to make decisions about some issues, you may need to become more informed. You may need information about taxes, about your legal rights, or about the value of your house, your business, or your pension plan. Your mediator should be able to refer you to competent professionals who can help you get the answers that you need in order to analyze your options.

- If you have minor children, an important question is how best to handle their care. Your mediator will assist you in creating a schedule which will meet everyone's needs as much as possible. Once you arrive at a plan that *looks* workable, you may want to try it out for a while, in order to see if it really works for the entire family.

- One of the benefits of mediation is that you can experiment with various parenting schedules until you find one that makes sense for your family. Start with a blank calendar and fill in time for the children to be with each of you. *Don't* begin with a preconceived idea based on what you have heard the court might order. Each family's needs are different.

- Throughout your mediation, as you gather information and search for solutions, you will enter into agreements which will eventually comprise your marital settlement agreement, a contract between the two of you, which sets forth your future rights and responsibilities.

- As the mediation continues, you and your spouse will work together to design a custom plan. It will be unlike any other couple's plan and unlike any that would have been imposed on your family, had you left these important issues to lawyers and judges to decide for you.

Twenty-Eight:
Full Disclosure--It's the Name of the Game

- One of the ground rules in divorce mediation is that each spouse must *voluntarily* disclose all assets and debts, as well as all income and expenses. In many states, disclosure is also required by law.

- People often fear that their spouse will hide an asset or fail to disclose some other important piece of financial information. They mistakenly believe that the whole truth will come out if lawyers pursue the case in court, but that only part of it will come out in mediation. The truth is that if someone is determined to withhold information, he or she can do so, whether the case is handled in court or in mediation. If you discover after the divorce that your spouse misrepresented the facts, you can ask the court to correct the situation, regardless of whether your divorce was litigated or mediated.

- The mediator's job is to help each spouse ask for all relevant information. In cases where either you or your spouse is unaware of what to ask for, the mediator will assist by telling each of you to bring certain documents to exchange at the mediation.

- A minimal level of trust between you and your spouse is necessary for a mediation to be successful. If either of you believes that he or she is getting only part of the truth, and can never get the whole truth, settlement negotiations are not likely to be productive.

- The final divorce agreement is usually referred to as a *"marital settlement agreement,"* a *"property settlement agreement,"* or a *"separation agreement."* This agreement should include a statement that each party has disclosed all financial matters to the other, *under penalty of perjury.* This language allows for appropriate penalties, in the event that either party intentionally fails to disclose all relevant information.

- Providing "full disclosure" regarding an asset usually means not only naming it, but also determining its value by reference to an outside, objective standard. All major assets should be appraised, unless you and your spouse have some other reliable way of establishing their value. Most couples agree to use only one expert to appraise each asset. One expert appraises the family business, another appraises the pension plans, and a third appraises the house and any other real estate. In most instances, getting outside input is the only way to obtain an objective opinion as to value. Once you have gathered this information, you can make informed decisions about how to divide your assets.

"Don't find fault, find a remedy."

Henry Ford

Twenty-Nine:
The Goal--A Level Playing Field

- In divorce mediation, unlike other types of mediation, most mediators do what they can to "balance the power" between the spouses.

- If either spouse appears to be negotiating from a weaker position, the mediator will attempt to empower that person, in order to create a more balanced outcome.

- Often one person is in a weaker position, because he or she has less *information*. When that is the case, the mediator usually recommends that the less informed spouse take specific steps to become more knowledgeable.

- If one spouse is uninformed about the family's finances, the mediator may suggest that he or she obtain outside assistance in order to get up to speed. With some expert help, the less informed spouse can usually return to the mediation equipped to negotiate from a more powerful position.

- In some instances, one spouse may feel inclined to waive important legal rights out of guilt. When this happens, the mediator usually recommends that he or she think about the *future* and make decisions that will seem fair in the years to come. Regardless of the circumstances leading up to the divorce, giving away the farm doesn't usually make sense in the long run.

- Mediators are trained to be supportive of each person's right to have an equal voice in the discussion of every issue. When one person is more aggressive than the other, the mediator may caucus with that individual and coach him or her in how to negotiate with more empathy.

- When one spouse is less assertive than the other, the mediator may take that individual into a caucus where they can discuss and role-play negotiating skills. With encouragement and practice, the weaker spouse can return to a joint session equipped to negotiate more forcefully and effectively.

- Most mediators establish ground rules in advance. Many include a rule that requires the husband and wife to listen to each other without interrupting. This prevents an aggressive spouse from controlling the process and ensures that a quiet spouse has a chance to voice his or her thoughts.

- Another common ground rule requires that the participants speak only for themselves, rather than attributing motives and feelings to each other. This communication tool helps balance the power and affirms that each spouse is responsible only for him or herself.

- In order for mediation to work, both spouses must feel free to say what they want, in an atmosphere where each person's views are respected. The mediator acts as a guide to the process and a referee when necessary. This ensures that each participant is treated respectfully and that decisions are made voluntarily, after thoughtful discussion of the implications to both spouses and to the children.

Thirty:
Understanding the Consequences of Your Decisions

- *Divorce*--the word itself evokes strong feelings. The process of getting divorced puts many people on an emotional roller coaster. Making decisions under these turbulent circumstances can be difficult.

- Should you give up control of your divorce to a lawyer just because you are emotionally overwrought? Not necessarily. In mediation you can take the time to gather all of the information that you need to make informed decisions. You can consult with outside experts, including an attorney, so that you are making each decision with your eyes wide open. Because the mediation process usually takes place over several months, you have an opportunity to get a handle on your emotions, with the aid of a professional counselor, if necessary.

- The mediator will help you consider the many ways of resolving each issue. Make sure that you have carefully weighed the pros and cons before deciding which solutions will work best for you. Go *slowly*. Once you sign a settlement agreement, it is too late to change your mind, except in child-related matters, which are *always* subject to modification.

- You may be tempted to give up your rights to your interest in a marital asset (for example, the family business) for a variety of reasons, including your desire to remain on friendly terms with your soon-to-be ex. Don't make hasty decisions. Instead, allow the mediator to help you evaluate the effect that each decision will have on your future financial security.

Can you afford to give up money to which you are entitled, in order to placate your spouse? What's the worst thing that could happen if you decided to stand up for your rights? Your mediator should support you in your efforts to obtain your fair share of the marital pie.

- Most mediators believe that each spouse has the right to make decisions for him or herself, whether or not the mediator agrees with the choice. In mediation, you are responsible for making your own decisions, after examining the consequences of each proposed agreement in light of your own needs.

- One good way to look at the decisions which you are considering is to ask yourself, "How will I feel about this five years from now?" The remorse which usually results from caving in to pressure or making a hasty decision can be avoided by taking all the time that you need to think things through, *before* you sign a settlement agreement. Don't let anyone rush you into deciding; insist on sufficient time to weigh your choices carefully.

"Mediation is a sleeping giant."

Frank E.A. Sander, Professor of Law

Thirty-One:
Using Attorneys as Consultants

- During divorce mediation, attorneys can play either a major or a minor role. Some couples who mediate their divorce choose not to involve attorneys at all.

- Most divorce mediators prohibit attorneys from attending the mediation sessions. On the other hand, they generally encourage or require each spouse to have the mediated agreement reviewed by a family law attorney prior to signing it. The reviewing attorneys act as consultants at the end of the process, double-checking the agreement to make sure that no issue is left unaddressed and that the legal ramifications are clear to both spouses.

- Some people feel that they want a lawyer on their side as they progress through the mediation sessions. These people often consult with a lawyer before starting mediation, as well as between sessions.

- Whether you use a lawyer frequently for consultations, or only at the end to review the proposed agreement, you should remember that the final decisions are *your* responsibility. Your lawyer will present options for settlement and offer opinions regarding what might happen if your case were to be decided by a judge. The final decisions still rest with *you*, and that's as it should be. *You*, not the attorney, will have to live with the consequences of your decisions.

- If you fail to reach a settlement with your spouse and have to handle the matter in court, *you*, not your attorney, will pay the price, in legal fees, in time, and in emotional energy.

- Be aware that your attorney may profit financially by raising your expectations and convincing you that you can get more in court than you can in a negotiated settlement. If you find yourself considering litigation, ask your lawyer for an estimate of the cost involved, including legal fees, and then review your options.

- Remember, when you use an attorney during a mediation, you are hiring a *consultant*. You are not obligated to follow his or her advice. Listen carefully to your attorney's recommendations, then follow only that advice which makes sense to you.

- Some mediators will speak with outside attorneys from time to time as the mediation progresses. Find out in advance if your mediator intends to do so, and if so, who pays the bill for the mediator's time. Ask your mediator to limit those contacts to conference calls in which you and your spouse, as well as both attorneys, can all be on the line together.

- Many mediators prepare all of the court paperwork that is required in order to complete your divorce. Mediators who are not attorneys generally do not do so. Instead, they prepare a *Memorandum of Understanding*, which forms the basis of the final settlement agreement. If your mediator does not complete all of the legal documents, you will need to hire a lawyer or a paralegal to draft the divorce papers. More about that in Chapter 38.

"It is wrong to waste the precious gift of time on acrimony and division."

Cardinal Joseph Bernardin

Thirty-Two:
Using Other Outside Experts

- Even a "simple" divorce can raise questions which the average person cannot answer. When those questions arise, mediators encourage their clients to get expert advice from outside professionals.

- One area where expert advice is often needed is taxes. Whether you intend to minimize taxes upon the sale of your home or to get the maximum tax advantage from your spousal support payments, an **accountant** can provide valuable information. Generally, it makes sense for you and your spouse to see an accountant together. However, if there is any question about the accountant's neutrality, you're each better off getting your own tax advice.

- If one of you is going to end up with a lump sum settlement, a **financial planner** can help. He or she can evaluate the tax ramifications and income-producing possibilities of such a settlement and advise you regarding future investments, as well.

- Because going through a divorce can feel like riding an emotional roller coaster, most people benefit from seeing a **counselor** or a **psychologist** during this turbulent period. Although a certain amount of emotional release takes place during mediation, mediation is not a substitute for therapy. Even if your mediator is a therapist, he or she can't wear *both* hats with the same client. Your mediation (and your life) will progress more smoothly, if you treat yourself to some sessions with a good therapist.

Additional Outside Resources

▸ **A bankruptcy attorney:** for information about the best way to structure an agreement when bankruptcy is anticipated.

▸ **A business appraiser:** for an appraisal of a family-owned business or interest in a professional practice.

▸ **A children's counselor:** for emotional problems that children may experience during divorce.

▸ **An insurance broker:** for assistance in purchasing new health, life, and casualty insurance policies.

▸ **A personal property appraiser:** for antiques, art, jewelry, and collections.

▸ **A pension appraiser:** for an appraisal of a defined benefit pension plan, when one spouse will retain the proceeds.

▸ **A psychiatrist or a primary care physician:** for antidepressants or other medications when indicated.

▸ **A real estate appraiser:** for appraisals of residential or commercial real estate.

▸ **A real estate broker:** for marketing and selling real estate.

▸ **A vocational counselor:** for assisting an unemployed spouse in exploring new career possibilities, as well as the education or training needed to enter the workplace.

Thirty-Three:
Replacing Custody Battles With Parenting Plans

- Children need *both* parents. Except in cases where one parent is abusive or unable to provide proper care and supervision, children benefit when both Mom and Dad play major roles in their lives. Mediation helps parents figure out how to manage child care under a totally new set of circumstances.

- Suggestion: Avoid the use of fighting words, such as "custody" and "visitation." These words set up a struggle over *possession* of the children.

- A more useful way for you to deal with the question of child care is to develop a *parenting plan* which describes the children's *schedule* with each of you. Your mediator will probably create this plan on a large, erasable wall calendar, asking for ideas as to when each of you would like to assume primary responsibility for the children's care.

- Once a tentative parenting plan is created, your family can try it out for a month or two, before deciding whether or not to include it in your settlement agreement. If parts of the plan need fine-tuning, you can discuss proposed changes, then revise your plan until it works smoothly for all involved.

- Some mediators permit older children to attend a mediation session to help with the parenting plan. If you decide to include your children, be sure that everyone understands the purpose of their participation. The children need to know that their input is important, but that you and your spouse will make the final decisions. Be careful not to put them in the difficult position of being asked which of you they want to live with.

- Any parenting plan that you and your spouse create is likely to work if you both support it. If you see potential problems with the plan as you proceed through the mediation, bring them up and correct them before you sign the final agreement.

- Remember, your children didn't cause the divorce. No matter what you do, they will pay a price for your decision to separate. However, it's up to *you* to keep that price as low as possible, even if it causes you inconvenience or decreases the amount of time that you spend with them.

- Put your children at the center of your focus and concentrate on their needs. Set a photo of your children in front of you and your spouse on the mediation table. Recognize that if you end up fighting over your rights to custody or visitation, rather than working out a plan with your spouse, the children will be the victims, regardless of which parent "wins."

- You and your spouse have the opportunity during mediation to cooperate in planning your children's future. Through careful planning, you can help your children view your family as *rearranged* into new homes, rather than torn apart and left in shreds.

- Consider making co-parenting agreements that will keep both you and your spouse involved in your children's lives and minimize the friction. Some examples appear on the following page.

Co-Parenting Agreements

1) Each parent agrees to have the children bathed, dressed, and fed, before the other one picks them up.

2) Each parent agrees to spend some time going over homework with the children, before returning them to the other parent.

3) One parent agrees to contact the schools and instruct them to send copies of all correspondence to both parents.

4) If one parent is shopping for the children's school clothes, the other agrees to shop for and purchase all clothing related to the children's extracurricular activities, including sports, scouts, etc.

5) Both parents agree to refrain from saying anything negative about the other within earshot of the children.

6) Both parents agree that the children should have a *real* home with each of them, and that neither should just have "visitation" with the children. Each parent provides a home that has some of the children's furniture, clothes, personal care items, games, and books.

7) Both parents agree to post a calendar in a place where the children can see it, showing everyone's schedule. With children too young to read, a *picture* of Mom or Dad on the calendar can indicate whose turn it is to take care of the them.

Flying the Friendly Skies

We mediated all of the usual divorce issues for Jeff and Judy and then approached the parenting plan, a sensitive subject, since they lived hundreds of miles apart. Both worked for the same airline; Jeff was a pilot and Judy was a flight attendant. Our discussion centered around their primary goal, which was to give their six-month old daughter, Wendy, a chance to share her formative years with each of them.

Using a wall calendar and their current schedules, we helped them create a 50-50 parenting plan which involved sending Wendy back and forth to each parent by plane, under the care of one of them or another flight attendant. Once the mediation was over, Jeff and Judy adjusted their schedules each month to meet their goal of equal time with Wendy. Each was willing to make the extra effort to cooperate and coordinate with the other, because they believed that the benefit to their child outweighed the sacrifices they had to make.

Mary Mudd Quinn, PhD, MFCC and Mediator
J. William Hargreaves, Attorney and Mediator

Thirty-Four:
Planning for Future Changes

- Even the most carefully thought out parenting plan is likely to need occasional revisions. The plan that you arrive at in mediation should be considered a *working draft,* subject to renegotiation if either of you wants to change it.

- As children get older, plans for their care and support often need to be revised. After arriving at a parenting plan and a support agreement in mediation, most people feel that they can negotiate adjustments by themselves; others return to mediation for help.

- As part of your Marital Settlement Agreement, you and your spouse should agree on a date, time, and place for a periodic planning meeting. This way you can revisit the issues of child support and the children's care and adjust them when necessary, on a regular basis.

- Your post-divorce planning meetings should be scheduled for at *least* once a year, more often if you prefer to plan for shorter time periods. Often the best time for a planning meeting is around May 1, after tax returns have been filed. You can hold the meeting by phone, by fax, via E-mail, or in person. Bring your calendars, the children's school calendars and athletic schedules, and anything else that will help you to prepare a schedule for several months in advance. Remember the need to remain flexible and to accommodate requests from each other for occasional changes.

- If you plan to discuss proposed changes in child support, bring tax returns, wage stubs, your state's child support guideline or formula, and information about your expenses. The subject of modifying support can be touchy. If you run up against roadblocks as you discuss changes in support, adjourn the meeting and set an appointment with your mediator.

- If substantial variations occur in your income or expenses, you may need to request a change in support, *before* your next scheduled meeting. Suggest to your spouse that if either of you has an increase or decrease in income by a certain percent (say ten or fifteen percent) or a sudden change in expenses related to the children, you will contact each other and set up an interim meeting.

Topics to Consider at Planning Meetings

- ► A child's request to change residence

- ► A child's request to alter the parenting plan

- ► Your desire (or need) to move

- ► Your change in income

- ► An increase/decrease in child-related expenses

- ► A proposed change of school

- ► Religious education

- ► Orthodontic/medical/dental expenses

- ► A child's extra-curricular activities

- ► College plans and costs

Thirty-Five:
Sparing the Children

- Fighting between parents can be the most damaging aspect of a divorce for children. Unfortunately, a court battle which focuses on custody places the children in the center of a conflict in which they are certain to be the losers.

- In mediation, you and your spouse have the opportunity to work together to focus on the needs of your children. You can demonstrate to them that the two of you are working *together* on a plan that will keep their lives as stable as possible.

- In mediation, you and your spouse can agree to refrain from fighting in front of the children and from saying negative things about each other within the children's earshot...ever.

- You can agree not to use the children as spies or messengers, regardless of how curious you are about your ex's lifestyle, and regardless of the convenience of sending messages via the children.

- You can focus on the children's needs for stability and predictability, by making sure that their school, their extracurricular activities, and the quality and extent of their contact with both of you change as little as possible.

- You can handle your own emotional issues by expressing your feelings and getting support in an adult setting, such as mediation or therapy. Then your children don't have to take care of *you* during your divorce.

The courts of this country should not be the place where the resolution of disputes begin. They should be the places where disputes end, after alternative methods of resolving disputes have been considered and tried. The courts of our various jurisdictions have been called the "court of last resort."

Justice Sandra Day O'Conner
U.S. Supreme Court

Thirty-Six:
Letting Go--The Emotional Divorce

- Most people go through a long grieving period when they realize that their marriage is ending. Mediation offers an opportunity to experience the emotional divorce concurrently with the legal divorce, by dealing with feelings, as well as facts.

- Divorcing couples often find themselves at opposite ends of the emotional spectrum. One person may be ready to move on with life, while the other remains in shock, unable or unwilling to believe that the marriage is really ending and a divorce is in progress.

- The two of you control the speed of the mediation process. At any time during the mediation, you can explore the possibility of getting back together. The mediation process should help each of you clarify whether or not you really want a divorce.

- Most mediators encourage couples to express their feelings about the divorce. This serves two purposes. It gets feelings out in the open, so that you can negotiate the factual issues in a more businesslike manner, and it allows you to lead healthier lives after the divorce, without the burden of unnecessary emotional baggage.

- People who go through a litigated divorce often end up angrier and more bitter after the divorce than they were when they started. Most people who mediate are able to bury the hatchet, making future contacts with the ex-spouse easier, a real benefit where children are involved.

"As you end your marriage and attempt to build a new life, it is vital to realize that your opponent is not your ex-spouse. Both of you, along with your children, face the same enemies--unchecked anger, corrosive fear, inadequate resources, uncertainty, and despair.

You will win or lose depending on what you do, on how well or poorly you accept and manage your own overwhelming feelings, and on how well or poorly you handle the irrational and potentially destructive behavior that may be displayed by your ex-spouse, your friends, your family, your adviser, and yourself."

Robert E. Adler

Thirty-Seven:
The Signing Ceremony

- Most of the important moments in our lives are marked by a ceremony. We have created rituals to celebrate birthdays, graduation, marriage, and the loss of a loved one. Why haven't we created divorce ceremonies to help us survive the demise of a marriage?

- Until the 1960's, divorces were the exception, not the norm. We didn't need divorce ceremonies, because most people remained married for a lifetime. Divorce was considered shameful, a sign of deep personal failure. Today, when half of all marriages result in divorce, we need divorce ceremonies to help us provide closure.

- Family mediators employ a variety of signing ceremonies. The ceremony is held on the day that the couple signs the Marital Settlement Agreement and other court documents. Once the legal documents are signed, the mediator invites the couple to participate in a brief ceremony, in recognition of the importance of this occasion in their lives.

- When no court appearance is required, the signing ceremony marks the end of the marriage for the couple, even though a judge's signature is technically the last step in the process. When a court appearance is required, the signing ceremony provides important emotional closure, even though it does not constitute the last step in the divorce process.

- Most couples invite parents and friends to share in their wedding ceremony. For the same reasons, some may want them to participate in their divorce signing ceremony. Friends and family can be invited to witness this rite of passage and to provide support and encouragement at a difficult time.

- Children can be invited to participate in the signing ceremony, too. They can prepare something to say or participate as observers. Their presence should be entirely voluntary.

- The signing ceremony provides an opportunity to demonstrate that although one relationship is over, another takes its place. Children, parents, and friends realize that they don't have to take sides or forego valuable relationships, simply because a divorce has occurred.

- When either spouse is still so angry or hurt about the divorce that a ceremony would be too painful, the mediator ends the final session as soon as the papers are signed, without any further ado.

"The promise of mediation is to transform conflict into resolution at its very core, rather than merely providing an answer to the superficial dispute."

Richard C. Reuben, Attorney

Sample Signing Ceremonies

Ceremony #1:   The mediator offers the husband and wife a glass of champagne or sparkling cider. Each spouse offers a toast, saying something positive about the past or the future. Then the mediator toasts the couple, congratulating them for working hard during the mediation, and acknowledging them for the gift that they have given to their children by deciding to mediate, instead of engaging in a court battle.

Ceremony #2:   In a ceremony held out-of-doors, the mediator unties a ribbon joining two helium balloons, as the couple watches. The mediator compares the balloons, as they drift apart into the sky, to the couple's lives, once closely tied together and now going in separate directions,

Ceremony #3: The mediator presents a cake with three candles. The husband and wife each light a side candle from the central candle, then extinguish the flame from the central candle. The mediator talks about the fact that although the couple's marriage is ending, a new life is beginning for each individual.

Ceremony #4: The mediator presents each parent with half of a key, telling them that they each hold half of the key to their children's future. The mediator then asks each parent to keep his or her half of the key, as a reminder that continuing to work together is essential for their children's happiness.

*"As part of the settlement, your wife is asking for
any three of the six letters of your surname.
You, of course, would retain the remaining three."*

Thirty-Eight:
Court Paperwork

- The amount of court paperwork required in a divorce varies from state to state. Some states ensure full employment for lawyers by requiring that each divorce document be drafted in the manner of a composition, instead of providing a form with boxes to check. Other states have simplified the process by creating forms that you can purchase at the courthouse; even these forms are difficult to fill out without assistance. In states where forms are not available, most couples, having neither the time nor the inclination to learn how to prepare legal documents themselves, pay an attorney to do so.

- You can expect that your mediator will either prepare the legal paperwork and file it with the court, or refer you to someone to do so. Some mediators work closely with paralegals or attorneys who will prepare and file the divorce documents on your behalf, without representing you.

- In a mediated divorce, the legal paperwork can be thought of as divided into three parts. Part I consists of the papers that initiate the divorce. These are usually called the *Summons* and *Petition* (or *Complaint*). When filed with the court, these papers instruct the clerk to open a divorce file.

- *Filing* is accomplished by handing documents to a clerk, who date-stamps them and puts them into a court file. Anyone can file a document, so long as it meets the court's standards. Most courts charge a fee to file the initial papers.

- In an adversarial divorce, attorneys generally file a *Response* to the Petitioner or Complaint. In a mediated divorce, this step is sometimes omitted, by agreement, while the parties are engaged in settlement discussions.

- Part II consists of the Marital Settlement Agreement ("MSA"). This document is sometimes referred to by other names, such as "Property Settlement Agreement," "Separation Agreement," or "Stipulated Judgment." When you and your spouse sign an MSA, it becomes a legally binding contract. After the judge signs it, the MSA takes on additional significance; it then becomes an official order of the court.

- Part III includes several documents. Sworn statements as to each party's income, expenses, assets, and debts must be exchanged, and in most cases filed with the court. A "Judgment" or "Order," gives the final divorce date and contains the most important agreements regarding the assets, the support, and the care of the children. The MSA, the Judgment, and the other court documents are usually filed together as soon as the mediation is concluded.

- Since the court's divorce files are usually open to public scrutiny, you should avoid including statements in them that you wouldn't want others to read, whenever possible.

- Make sure that the person who files your divorce papers with the court gives the clerk a copy of each document to stamp and return to you for your permanent records.

Thirty-Nine:
Court Appearances

- In most states, the law still requires that for a divorce to become final, one party must appear in court at a "default hearing" or "prove-up hearing" to answer a series of simple questions that the judge poses. Either your mediator or an attorney should be able to provide you with a list of the usual questions, along with the responses that you will be expected to give.

- The judge's questions are aimed at establishing your place of residence, your decision to get divorced, and your understanding of your agreement.

Sample Questions

- ▸ Have you lived in this state for [some number of] months and in this county for [some number of] months?

- ▸ Would counseling help to preserve this marriage?

- ▸ Have you read your Marital Settlement Agreement?

- ▸ Do you understand all of its terms?

- ▸ Do you choose to be bound by your Agreement?

- If you live in a state where a court appearance is required, consider attending the hearing with your spouse. The two of you attended the wedding ceremony together. It makes sense that you both be present as the marriage is officially ended.

- If you have to go to court, your mediator may be willing to go along for moral support. Whether or not your mediator attends, you can ask a family member or a friend to go with you. This may be an emotional occasion, so plan ways to get through it as easily as possible.

- In some states, such as California, a court appearance is not required. In these states, you or your mediator can send your divorce papers to the court. The judge will review them, and sign them if everything is in order. Instead of mailing your papers to the court, you can go to the courthouse and deliver them to the clerk yourself. Either way, it may take several days or weeks before your documents are processed by the clerk and signed by the judge. If you provide an extra set of copies as well as a self-addressed, stamped envelope, the clerk will send your signed papers back to you, with the judge's signature and the date that your divorce became final.

- If your state requires a personal appearance to obtain a divorce, the next time that you hear anyone complaining about crowded courts, remind them that time is wasted each day when judges question people who have already agreed to the terms of their divorce, asking if they meant what they said in their papers and if they knew what they were doing when they made their decisions. Ask, "What's the point of requiring a court appearance when many states have demonstrated that divorces can be handled by mail?"

Section 3 -- *WHEN THINGS GO SOUR IN THE WORKPLACE*

Forty:
Somebody Broke a Contract

- Whether your small business hired someone to fix a fax machine and it died the following day, or your large corporation purchased a million dollars worth of computer chips which proved to be defective, you've got a problem that needs to be resolved quickly and inexpensively. If the other side won't cooperate in resolving the problem directly, you will probably think twice before bringing a lawsuit, because litigation will be too costly and slow. If you know how to use mediation, you can pursue resolution of your dispute, while preserving your relationship with the other side.

- Depending on the amount of money at stake, you may or may not decide to involve a lawyer in mediation. If your company employs a staff of attorneys, the decision is easy. Otherwise, you should determine whether the dispute is one that you can handle yourself, or whether the expense of hiring a lawyer to help prepare for and assist you during the mediation is warranted. If the stakes are high, you should retain an attorney. In addition, you may decide to enlist the help of your accountant, an expert in the subject matter of the dispute, or a business associate with first-hand knowledge of the situation. If this is your first mediation, you're better off with at least one other person on your team.

- The best way to initiate mediation is first to identify and contact two or three mediators who have experience with mediation in the area of your dispute. You can do so by calling the referral sources or the mediators listed in the Directory in the back of this book. You can also get names of mediators by looking in the Yellow Pages under *MEDIATION*, or by asking a lawyer or a colleague for a referral.

- The next step is to contact the individual or company that you believe broke your contract and tell them that you want to resolve the problem quickly, with the help of a mediator. Give them the names and phone numbers of the mediators that you have contacted, and ask them to phone each of them and then get back to you by a specific date. Alternatively, you may ask the mediator to contact the other side for you.

- Once you and the other side have agreed on the best mediator for the job and on the portion of the mediator's fee that each side will pay, you can set a date for the mediation and begin your preparation. Before embarking on that task, read Chapter Forty-Four, which describes eight ways to prepare for a successful workplace mediation.

- Plan ahead. Before continuing with business as usual, make sure that each contract that you intend to use in the future contains a paragraph that *requires* the use of mediation in disputes that arise from that agreement. An example of such a paragraph appears on page 99.

Forty-One:
So Your Boss is Picking on You

- If you're having problems at work, don't delay, take action! You and everyone else will be better off if you address the problem as soon as possible. Waiting will only make things worse.

- If your boss has created an atmosphere which fosters open communication and encourages problem solving, you may be able to negotiate a resolution to the issue yourself, without involving a third party.

- On the other hand, if you can't find an effective problem-solving avenue within your company, look outside for help. Try mediation first, and if that doesn't work, consider binding arbitration.

- If you have been sexually harassed, wrongfully terminated, unfairly evaluated, or mistreated in some other way, and have experienced no relief through the usual channels, you should select a mediator who handles employment issues.

- Also consider enlisting the assistance of an attorney who is experienced in employment law. The fact that you have a lawyer on your team may send a message to your employer that you really mean business.

- You or your attorney should contact several mediators who are experienced in employment disputes, and then select the one that you feel the most comfortable with. Ask that mediator to contact your employer to set up a mediation.

Requests for Termination Benefits

1. Continuation of your salary for a specified time
2. Continuation of your insurance benefits
3. Employer-provided letter of reference
4. Mutually agreed upon internal communication as to your departure
5. Employer-paid out-placement service
6. Employer-paid resume service
7. Employer-paid image counseling service
8. Employer-paid career counseling services
9. Employer-paid health club for a specified time
10. Employer-paid psychological counseling for you and your family
11. Employer-paid child care services for a specified time during your job search
12. Employer-paid administrative support services (telephone, fax, e-mail, etc.) for a specified time during out-placement transition
13. Continuation of your current professional training program
14. Continuation of your scheduled professional seminar/or conference plan for a specified time
15. Employer-paid professional dues or memberships for a specified time
16. Forgiveness of any outstanding loan balance (real estate purchases, relocation assistance) or obligation to repay a sign-on bonus

Forty-Two:
You've Got the Employee from Hell

- In virtually every workplace, conflicts arise which lead to disputes between workers or between the company and its employees. In spite of enlightened personnel policies and modern management techniques, disputes with employees are bound to arise.

- It's tempting to ignore conflicts with employees. Unfortunately, however, unresolved conflicts don't just evaporate; they usually resurface with renewed urgency at a later time. A disgruntled employee is more likely to take sick leave, perform at a minimal level, and/or contaminate the work environment with negativity. The longer that you allow an employee's negative feelings to fester, the more difficult, time-consuming, and expensive your job will eventually be when you are forced to address the problem.

- Minor conflicts can often be ironed out informally. Mediation is more apt to be required when you need to resolve a major dispute, the kind that occurs when an employee believes that he or she has been fired unfairly, given an unjust performance evaluation, or subjected to sexual harassment. Left unresolved, this type of dispute can erupt into a lawsuit that can damage your company's morale, its public image, and its bank balance.

- Mediation is particularly useful in disputes where strong emotions are present, because the key players are required to air their feelings and address the issues face-to-face, in a controlled environment, rather than gathering ammunition and preparing for warfare.

90

- An employee who feels injured must be free to tell his or her side of the dispute, because venting and being heard are critical aspects of the mediation process. Although you may have to listen to your employee blame you for what has happened, he or she will also be required to listen to *your* side of the story. At some point, the mediator will ask each side to state the other's point of view. After this occurs, the focus usually shifts from mutual blaming to searching for solutions that will meet everyone's needs. With the assistance of a creative mediator, you should be able to settle even the most difficult workplace dispute in a session or two.

- Before you return to business as usual, take some time out to write down the steps that you want to follow when disputes with employees arise in the future. If you already have an employee manual, revise it. On page 99 you will find two paragraphs that you should include in employee contracts.

Practical Pointers

▸ Insist that each decision-maker participates, including the employee's spouse.

▸ Try to step into your employee's shoes and understand his or her view of the problem.

▸ Keep an open mind regarding new options.

▸ Identify your next best alternative to a negotiated settlement and estimate its cost.

▸ Determine how far you are willing to go to meet your employee's demands.

Forty-Three:
Why Bother with Mediation?

- By using mediation to resolve disputes in the work-place, you can save a great deal of *time* for more profitable pursuits. The average mediation takes less than a week, saving you months or years in which to focus on making a profit, instead of on developing your litigation strategy.

- By using mediation you can dramatically reduce your *legal fees*. Whether the mediation takes a few hours or a few days, the fees that you pay to both the mediator and your attorney will usually be less than the cost of a day of deposition or trial.

- If you opt for mediation, you have *no downside risk*, other than the relatively minimal expense of the mediation. If you fail to reach a settlement, you can still proceed with an arbitration or a trial. By using mediation, you avoid the risk that a judge or jury will rule against you. You foreclose the possibility of getting hit with an outrageous verdict at trial, one which forces you either to accept a huge loss or to spend more time and money pursuing the possibility of a better result through an appeal.

- When you negotiate a settlement in mediation, your company's internal matters remain *private*, out of the public view.

- Perhaps most important, a successful mediation may allow you to maintain a positive relationship with the other side in the future, a benefit which often outweighs the stakes in the current dispute.

Home Sweet Home

Larry had worked as a funeral director in a small town funeral home for 26 years, when the owners accused him of making suggestive sexual comments to another employee. Outraged at the accusation, Larry countered his employer's claim with a demand for three years of back overtime pay. The employer agreed to mediate and wisely invited Larry's wife, Laverne, to participate. Larry and Laverne were engaged in their own dispute: Larry was determined not to return to his job and refused to apologize for his comments; Laverne wanted to continue living in the funeral home, the only home that their 14-year old daughter had ever known.

During the mediation, all of the participants had an opportunity to air their feelings. After everyone was heard, they arrived at a plan which satisfied each of them. The company agreed to let Larry and his family live in the home for 2½ years, while he completed his studies for an embalmer's license, at their expense. They also agreed to pay a lump sum to cover his salary during his schooling, as well as six months of additional salary to give Larry a chance to find a new job. Larry resigned and withdrew his claim for back pay, as requested. Laverne continued her part-time work as a hairdresser for the corpses. Everyone agreed to keep the terms of the settlement confidential.

Herman Wacker, Attorney and Mediator

Forty-Four:
Eight Ways to Prepare for a Successful Workplace Mediation

1) Gather all *paperwork* that pertains to the dispute and organize it chronologically in a divided file folder. Make copies for each participant in the mediation.

2) Determine whether or not you need *assistance* in handling your side of the dispute. If you plan to involve others, get them on board early, so that you can prepare as a team.

3) Consult with one or more *attorneys* to find out what might happen if your case went to court. They will probably differ in their analyses, so you should get a *range* of estimates. Keep in mind that the answers you get from lawyers represent only one way of looking at how to resolve your dispute. In mediation, you and the other side may find that your best solutions are far more inventive than those envisioned by the law.

4) Plan, then *rehearse*, your recital of the facts as you see them. At the beginning of the mediation, each person will be invited to give his or her synopsis of what happened. If visual aids will clarify your presentation, prepare them and practice incorporating them into your remarks.

5) Make a list of your *underlying interests*. An interest is not a position or a stand, but rather a statement of your needs. Don't leave anything out. Number the items from most important to least important. The chances of your reaching a settlement that includes your *entire* wish list is remote, so establish your priorities ahead of time. Stay flexible, and open to new ideas.

6) Attempt to anticipate the *other side's needs*. What will be on *their* wish list? Which of those wishes would you be willing to grant in order to resolve the dispute and move on? Try to predict their requests and their priorities.

7) Consider your *alternatives* to a mediated settlement and identify the costs connected with each. Factor in the cost of the time that you and others in your company will devote to the dispute, if you fail to settle it.

8) Write a succinct summary of the facts in the dispute from your perspective, and submit it to your mediator several days in advance of the mediation. If an attorney is assisting you, he or she can draft a "Mediation Brief," describing your version of the facts and citing the law that applies to your case. Although a brief is not normally required in a mediation, it can help by providing the mediator with valuable background information.

"In a real sense all life is interrelated. All men are caught in an inescapable network of mutuality, tied in a single garment of destiny. Whatever affects one directly affects all indirectly. I can never be what I ought to be until you are what you ought to be, and you can never be what you ought to be until I am what I ought to be."

Martin Luther King, Jr.

Forty-Five:
Preventing Personnel Disasters

- Because the cost of litigation is so staggering, any effort that proves successful in preventing workplace lawsuits can add thousands, or even millions, of dollars to your company's bottom line each year.

- Even small businesses need a plan for dealing with personnel conflicts. No business, small or large, can afford to waste valuable resources defending against a lawsuit that could have been reframed by a mediator into a cooperative search for mutually advantageous solutions.

- One way to insure that personnel disputes are resolved at the lowest level is to require that each person in the company agrees in writing to follow your conflict resolution procedure before taking legal action. The procedure should be easy to initiate and free of cost to the employee. You may want to employ a professional to design such a system.

Basic Dispute Resolution Steps

1. Try resolving the problem directly.

2. Involve an outside mediator to facilitate agreement.

3. Submit the matter to an arbitrator, one with no links to either side, for binding arbitration.

A QuickCheck for Employers

For those business owners who want to determine if a dispute management system is necessary, conduct this simple QuickCheck survey.

● stop ● look ● listen

Stop and check your personnel records to see if everyone has taken all of their sick leave and vacation time. Determine how often employees leave the company. Listen to how your employees talk to one another. If everyone has taken all of their days off, if no one is remaining with the organization very long, or if there are many negative discussions around the office, this may indicate a workplace with damaging disputes. These are only indicators.

If there is only one indicator, continue to monitor the situation. If there are two or three problematic areas, investigate further.

Nancy Neal Yeend
Dispute Management Specialist

Forty-Six:
Preventing Contract Catastrophes

- Contract catastrophes occur when one party concludes that the other is not living up to the terms of their contract and that they are unable to negotiate a resolution to the problem on their own. In most such cases, the contract itself suggests no clear-cut path to resolving the dispute collaboratively.

- Many contracts call for arbitration in the event of a dispute. Although this type of provision is better than no provision for dispute resolution, arbitration should generally be reserved for cases where mediation has been attempted unsuccessfully.

- All contracts should provide for systematic steps to be followed by both sides in case of a dispute. The first step should be direct negotiation, the second mediation, and the third, *binding* arbitration. If you want to retain the right to appeal the arbitrator's decision, choose *non-binding* arbitration instead.

- A modern approach to preventing and managing contract disputes is called "partnering." Partnering is a process where individuals or entities which intend to do business together meet and anticipate problems which may arise from their new venture. The meetings are usually conducted by a facilitator, using mediation principles. The participants negotiate a plan to prevent controversies and design a process to follow, should disputes arise. The purpose of partnering is to design ways to prevent disputes and then to constructively manage them, if they arise, so that they can be resolved as quickly as possible.

Mediation and Arbitration Paragraphs To Include in (Almost) Every Contract

In the event that a dispute arises regarding any matter contained in this agreement, the parties will first seek resolution of that dispute through mediation. If they are unable to agree on the selection of a mediator, they shall each select one mediator, and those two mediators shall in turn select a third to mediate the dispute. The cost of mediation shall be borne equally by the parties [or paid in full by _____].

In the event that the parties fail to resolve any dispute relating to this agreement by means of mediation, the dispute shall be settled by binding arbitration in [_____ city _____] in accordance with rules proposed by the arbitrator and acceptable to the parties. Judgment upon the award rendered by the arbitrator may be entered in any court having jurisdiction over the matter. The prevailing party shall be entitled to recover reasonable attorney's fees.

Section 4 -- *DEALING WITH LIFE'S OTHER CATASTROPHES*

Forty-Seven:
Settling Insurance Claims

- What's wrong with this picture? You are rear-ended by another driver, your five-year-old car is totaled, and you suffer back and neck injuries which render everything that you do painful. Your insurance company offers what they say is sufficient money to buy a similar car, but *your* car was in almost perfect condition, and you cannot replace it for the amount that they are offering. To make matters worse, the other driver's insurance company is willing to pay you only a few hundred dollars more than your doctor bills, despite the fact that you have spent the last year getting x-rays, going to therapy, taking pain pills, and missing out on all the things that you used to enjoy doing. Your choices, according to your lawyer, are: 1) settle for far less than you think you deserve, or 2) spend the next year or two waiting for a court-room and take your chances at trial. Your lawyer will get a third of your recovery if you settle out of court, and a higher percentage if you go to trial.

- For years, many insurance companies have paid sub-stantial fees to their defense lawyers to engage in legal tactics designed to disclaim responsibility, rather than to resolve disputes. The goal has been to give the claimant as little money as possible and to postpone payment for as long as possible.

- In the typical case, neither the insurance company, the defense attorney, nor the plaintiff's attorney pushes for an early settlement. Instead, the insurance company pays out large sums of money to its defense lawyers, money that might otherwise go to the injured party. Both sides engage in extensive pretrial fact-finding, spending hours seeking answers to endless questions, many of which will have little or no effect on the eventual outcome of the case. The cost of this "discovery" is borne by the injured party, as well as by the rest of the insurance company's policy holders.

- Our judicial system does not require litigants to discuss settlement at the earliest opportunity. Rather, judges hold settlement conferences a few weeks prior to trial, in hopes of clearing their over-booked calendars. By this time, the injured party has put in so much time getting ready for trial that he or she is often not in the mood to compromise.

- Instead of waiting for the court to schedule a settlement conference, the parties should attempt an early resolution by engaging the assistance of a mediator. The odds are better than 50-50 that the case will settle at the mediation. Money will be saved by the company, as well as by the taxpayers, a group that always pays the price when litigants use the resources of the court.

- If you are the victim of someone else's careless driving or other negligent conduct, you can save yourself a lot of time and trouble by requesting mediation at the *earliest possible time*. Schedule a mediation as soon as your condition becomes "permanent and stable." Once you have gathered enough information about the likelihood of incurring future medical bills or other accident-related expenses, including lost wages, you are ready to mediate.

- The sooner you resolve your case, the sooner you can focus on getting well. As long as you have to remain ready to testify at trial regarding your pain and suffering, you can't afford to recover fully and to move on with your life.

- By settling your personal injury case as soon as practicable through mediation, you can enjoy numerous advantages which are not available to those who choose to litigate their case:

    1) You get a sum of money that you can live with, instead of facing the possibility of a zero verdict from a judge or jury.

    2) You get your money sooner, rather than later.

    3) You don't have to worry about going through a trial where you will be subjected to the stress of being cross-examined on the witness stand.

    4) You won't have to take time off from work to prepare for a deposition, an arbitration, or a trial.

    5) You can focus all of your energy on getting your health back; instead of on keeping your injuries and pain foremost in your mind, so that you can describe them to a jury.

- Following natural disasters, such as hurricanes, floods, and earthquakes, insurance companies have found that they can minimize their legal costs and meet their insureds' needs for fair and speedy settlements by handling claims through mediation.

- Many personal injury attorneys and insurance claims adjusters don't understand that the injured party may have needs that go beyond money. Often, a sincere *apology* from the individual, company, or government agency responsible for the accident is a good place to start. A statement by the defendant about corrective steps that are being taken to prevent a similar accident in the future may also help. For instance, a city manager might explain that a stop sign is being installed at the intersection where the plaintiff was injured. The defendant driver might apologize for not being more watchful.

- Once people's intangible needs are met, a financial agreement can be worked out more easily. The plaintiff may be satisfied with less money, if his or her intangible needs are addressed.

- Creative settlement packages, such as those frequently crafted in mediation, may put the client at odds with the needs of his or her attorney. A settlement which includes intangibles may appeal to the plaintiff, but may not satisfy the plaintiff's lawyer. One-third of an apology, or of a promise to rectify a dangerous condition, won't pay the attorney's rent. Choose your attorney carefully, and pick one who has *your* best interests at heart. Consider retaining an attorney on an hourly, rather than a contingency, fee basis.

The average American during his or her lifetime will be involved in five major legal battles. These will involve buyer versus seller, tenant versus seller, tenant versus landlord, driver versus driver, husband versus wife, and insured versus insurance company.

Forty-Eight:
Ironing Out Problems with Neighbors

- A few years ago, an attorney and his neighbor spent $40,000 fighting in court over the exact location and height of the fence between their properties. At the end of the lawsuit, they hated each other so much that one of them sold his home and moved. More often, people who are angered by a neighbor's conduct suffer in silence. Even though their peace of mind is at stake, they don't want to wage a court battle or pay a lawyer to resolve a conflict that doesn't involve money.

- Common problems between neighbors include disputes over unruly children, barking dogs, loud music, late-night parties, abandoned vehicles, overhanging shrubs and trees, fences in need of repair or replacement, barriers to a view, upkeep of landscaping, disposal of garbage, maintenance of shared driveways, etc., etc., etc. Whatever the problem, mediation can provide speedy relief in situations such as these, where feelings run high.

- The best place to turn for a solution to your problem with a neighbor is a community dispute resolution center. Because most of these centers are publicly funded and staffed by trained volunteers, they provide free or low-cost mediation services.

- If you call and request a mediation, the intake staff will usually contact the other side and make the necessary arrangements for mediation to begin. All you need to do is show up, ready to tell your side of the story, and assist in the search for solutions.

Silence is Bliss

Mr. Wright was infuriated at Ms. Barker, because her dogs barked incessantly and used his yard for a bathroom. A retired Navy man, Mr. Wright believed that he had earned the right to enjoy some peace and quiet in his own garden. In mediation, he complained that Ms. Barker had trained her dogs to leave droppings on his side of their fence and allowed them to bark at him while he was gardening. Ms. Barker countered that Mr. Wright had squirted her dogs with a hose.

The mediators explored the neighbors' common interests. Mr. Wright and Ms. Barker learned that both had moved to their town reluctantly from other states, and that both had chosen a warm, inland climate, over the dampness of the coast.

As the mediation progressed, Mr. Wright agreed to go over to Ms. Barker's yard and be introduced to her dogs. Ms. Barker agreed to move the dog run to the other side of her yard, away from Mr. Wright's garden. Mr. Wright agreed to stop yelling at Ms. Barker and to write her a note, if the problem continued. Two months later, both of them reported satisfaction with their agreement, including two unexpected benefits: Ms. Barker was enjoying her view of Mr. Wright's garden, and, as a neighborly gesture, Mr. Wright had given Ms. Barker some of his home-grown vegetables.

Liz O'Brien, San Diego Mediation Center

Forty-Nine:
Fixing Broken Promises--
Landlords, Loans, and Lemons

- You've moved everything out of the old house, cleaned until it was spotless, given proper notice, and now your landlord won't return your deposit. You have your before and after pictures and eighteen witnesses lined up for court. *Before* you file a small claims action, call your local dispute resolution center. They'll call the landlord and arrange for a mediation. Perhaps this mess can be settled in an hour or two, without raising anyone's blood pressure.

- You bought a used car from your neighbor's cousin for $10,000. Even though the car had lots of miles on it, the seller swore that the engine had been re-built three months ago. Two weeks after you bought the car, the engine died and now the seller says that he can't help you. Before you call an attorney, think of the money and time and sleeplessness that a legal battle will cost. Your nearest non-profit dispute resolution center may be able to help you reach a reasonable settlement.

- You loaned $5000 to Uncle Harry. Things were great then--your business was booming and you had extra cash. Now you really need that $5000 back, but Uncle Harry just told you he can't repay you. Rather than going ballistic, see if a mediator can help you and Uncle Harry figure out creative ways that he can pay you back, like giving you a few weeks in his time share or raising cash by selling his racing motorcycle.

New Lawyer Disillusioned

Relieved to have finally completed all of the steps to becoming an attorney, I received my first issue of the Bar Journal and was utterly disgusted by the display of "important trials." I noted the two similarities between each of the listed cases. In each case the plaintiff won, and in each case summary there is the notation "Award: $..."

Is this what makes a trial important? Is it called an "award" because it's like a prize or a trophy? I thought plaintiffs were supposed to be compensated, not given a prize.

The underlying problem with the tort system is that it shifts the blame to the deepest pocket and justifies that transfer. We live in a society that believes in entitlements and refuses to accept responsibility for its own actions.

California Attorney

Fifty:
Disputes over Real Estate Sales

- A transaction as seemingly simple as buying or selling a house can turn into a nightmare. Despite efforts on both sides to identify potential problems, someone often ends up disappointed and angry.

- As a rule, buyers and sellers are not permitted by their real estate agents to communicate with each other outside of the agents' presence. When a dispute arises, they have no easy way of resolving it directly. Frustrated and suspicious, they often turn to the courts, the only option they can think of.

- In most instances, the amount of money at stake in a residential real estate dispute does not warrant the expense of litigation. Even if you're sure you will win, your legal fees may exceed your recovery and may not be paid by the other side.

- If you are involved in a real estate dispute, whether it's over a two-bedroom house or a ten-acre shopping mall, initiate mediation as soon as you realize that you cannot resolve the dispute yourself through direct negotiation. Urge the real estate agents, along with any others who were involved in the transaction, such as the escrow officer or the attorneys who handled the closing, to participate too. Make sure that everyone knows that you are proposing mediation as an *alternative* to a lawsuit, and that everyone understands that by contributing a small amount of money toward resolving the dispute through mediation, they may avoid paying the high cost of litigation.

A View from the Bench

My personal commitment to promoting facilitative mediation stems from actual experience with the process and the belief that it works well. It is easy to recognize that parties have a greater desire to resolve their "interests" promptly and cost effectively than they do in continuing an expensive and time consuming legal discussion regarding their "rights."

In such emotional and legally complex cases as those involving easements, or claims of adverse possession, or other claims involving real property, our Court has seen facilitative mediation produce prompt, satisfactory case resolution by having the parties sit down and discuss their competing interests early in the litigation. The parties themselves craft successful resolutions, which is important, as they often continue to enjoy a relationship as neighbors. The greatest current impediment to the increased use of facilitative mediation has been communicating with and educating attorneys regarding a dispute resolution process which is quite different than the litigation model which they studied in law school.

Judge Philip E. Rodgers, Jr.
Circuit Court Judge
Traverse City, Michigan

Fifty-One:
Prenuptial Agreements--
Negotiating Your Marriage Contract

- Increasingly, couples begin their marriage with a written contract. The usual reason for taking such a businesslike approach to marital rights and responsibilities is the desire to protect assets with high financial or sentimental value from being characterized as marital property, in the event of death or divorce.

- Traditionally, one person engages a lawyer to draft the prenuptial agreement, and the other hires a different lawyer to review it. Although the process may *begin* amicably, the negotiations often become volatile and lead to angry confrontations and lack of trust between the soon-to-be spouses. Occasionally, the hostility becomes so intense that wedding plans are abandoned altogether.

- You and your fiancé can approach your prenuptial agreement as a cooperative venture, instead of an adversarial nightmare, by hiring a mediator, or better yet, a male-female team of mediators, to help you through this highly sensitive negotiation.

- Once a preliminary agreement is drafted by your mediators, each of you should have it reviewed by outside counsel. Involving an attorney as a *consultant,* rather than as your representative, costs less and evokes less distrust than does using an attorney to negotiate and draft the agreement.

- Although traditional prenuptial agreements deal solely with financial issues, mediated prenuptial agreements often include other areas of concern as well. For instance, you may want to discuss the role that each of you will play as step-parents. In addition, you may decide to address questions regarding division of household chores, expectations regarding time spent with the in-laws, or the use of your leisure time.

- During the process of mediating your prenuptial agreement, you will inevitably learn more about negotiating with each other, a skill that should serve you well during your marriage.

Topics to Consider

- *Ownership of marital and premarital assets*
- *Responsibility for marital and premarital debts*
- *Division of household duties*
- *Division of parenting responsibilities*
- *Joint and/or separate bank accounts*
- *Responsibility for household expenses*
- *Joint or separate tax returns*
- *Expectations regarding free time*
- *Expectations regarding in-laws*
- *Ownership of inheritances*
- *Financial obligations to children and step-children*

Fifty-Two:
Making Changes After Divorce

- The courts are jammed with parents who want to change child custody, visitation, and support. Some go to court because they don't know any other way to make changes; others go because they have not finished their emotional divorce and are using the courtroom as a battlefield in their ongoing effort to wound each other. Whatever your motive, returning to court is usually the slowest, most expensive, least satisfactory way to change your divorce decree.

- If you wish to modify the terms of your divorce, make a *direct request* of your ex for the change that you want. Offer something that you are willing to give in return. Usually a letter works best, because it gives the recipient time to think before responding. If your request is rejected, ask your ex to meet and discuss the matter with you and a mediator.

- If custody and visitation are the issues to be resolved, you should approach mediation prepared to discuss specific times when each of you can be responsible for your children. Absent circumstances where one parent is neglectful or abusive, children need time with *both* parents. Don't expect the mediator to determine which of you is the better parent; that's not the mediator's job, and it just wastes time.

- You may want to plan one month as a trial period. If that month works smoothly, use the mediator's help in planning the next three to six months, as well as holidays and vacations for the rest of the year. Soon you should be able to work out schedules yourselves.

Better Endings

Mike and Susan returned to mediation three years after their divorce was final, having hit a snag. They were both angry and prepared to do battle in court, if necessary. Mike claimed that Susan owed him $127,000 as her share of the expenses he had incurred in selling their home following the divorce.

Susan revealed that she had felt pressured when Mike insisted that she sign the real estate sale documents, without enough time for her to have them reviewed by her attorney. Mike explained how frustrated he felt when he realized that the sale might fall through, if Susan refused to sign the papers. After Mike and Susan expressed their feelings to each other, each was directed by the mediators to restate what he or she understood the other to say. When they finally managed to step into each other's shoes and view the sale proceedings from the other's vantage point, a radical shift occurred. They let go of their rigid positions and listened to each other's requests. The financial issues became manageable. With comparative ease, the mediators helped Mike and Susan reach an agreement: Susan agreed to pay Mike $54,000 and to cooperate with him regarding disputed tax issues, a resolution which both considered fair.

Fifty-Three:
Victim-Offender Mediation

- Victim-offender mediation begins the healing process for the victim, the victim's family, and the offender. It is a voluntary process for all involved.

- Most victim-offender mediation programs are sponsored by churches, community organizations, or probation departments. They usually provide free or low cost mediations to the participants.

- The mediation process usually begins when offenders are referred to mediation by police or probation. Most victim-offender programs work with juveniles who have committed either nonviolent property offenses or misdemeanor assaults. A small number of adult offenders do post-conviction mediation for serious felonies. In these cases, the mediation is generally requested by the victim or the victim's family. It does not serve to reduce the offender's sentence.

- In most victim-offender mediations, a restitution agreement is worked out and signed. Offenders benefit by seeing the victim as a real person whom they have hurt and by being given the opportunity to make restitution for their crime.

- Victims benefit by being able to ask questions such as, "Why me?" The process helps victims reduce their anger, frustration, and fear. Often blind rage at a nameless, faceless offender is replaced by an understanding of the circumstances which led up to the offense, as well as some sense of peace and closure.

Lawyers and judges should be leaders in helping the public realize that imprisonment is expensive and relatively ineffective over the long haul. We should also be leaders in teaching non-coercive conflict resolution techniques, but first we need to learn them ourselves.

Judge Anne Kass
Second Judicial District
Albuquerque, New Mexico

Fifty-Four:
Kids and School Mediation

- Society benefits when students learn nonviolent ways of dealing with disputes. Young people who learn conflict resolution skills in school are able to make better choices when faced with difficult situations at home and in the community.

- Conflict resolution programs in schools have taught children and staff to:

    1. Take responsibility for their own actions.
    2. Identify and focus on the problem.
    3. Attack the *problem* not the *person.*
    4. Respect each individual's feelings.
    5. Listen with an open mind.

- The primary goal of these programs is to train students to help each other deal with anger effectively and manage their conflicts peacefully.

- The staff benefits, because they spend less time settling disputes among students.

- Students benefit by gaining leadership skills, enhancing self-esteem, and learning problem-solving techniques.

- Families experience a decrease in friction at home when children who have learned conflict management skills at school apply those techniques in their everyday lives.

I'll Scratch Your Eyes Out

Two female students almost got into a fight in the hallway of their school. After being separated, they were given the choice of either resolving the dispute through peer mediation or accepting staff consequences for the incident. Both students agreed to try peer mediation, because they were eager to confront each other. The student mediator began by introducing herself and setting the ground rules, which included that she would remain neutral, would keep the process confidential, and would not permit interruptions, put-downs, or threats.

As Clara told her story, it became clear that she was angry because she had heard that Janelle had gone to Clara's boyfriend and told him things that she had shared with Janelle in confidence. The mediator asked Janelle to restate Clara's feelings about the incident. Janelle said, "She felt betrayed, just like I did when she went to my boyfriend." The mediator pointed out that the girls had two things in common. They had felt betrayed when a private conversation was reported to a third party, and they were not going to put up with any b.s. from anyone. Eventually, the girls worked on solutions. They agreed to keep their conversations with each other about boys to themselves, to ask the other person's permission before repeating private remarks, and to resolve future problems with each other by talking it out, rather than resorting to fighting.

Andrew Margolin, Clinical Psychologist

Section 5 -- *NEGOTIATING YOUR BEST DEAL*

Fifty-Five:
Competitive vs. Cooperative Negotiation

- There are many types of negotiators. Two distinctive types are the competitive negotiator and the cooperative negotiator. Both employ useful techniques. Knowing how to identify their strategies will help you succeed in a mediation.

- A **competitive negotiator** wants to achieve a one-sided win and employs the following tactics:

    1) Starts with a demand that is unrealistically high or low.

    2) Insists that the other side is at fault, denies any responsibility, and uses threats.

    3) Demands that the negotiation take place on his or her home turf.

    4) Uses time to advantage: "This offer is good only until 5:00 p.m. tomorrow."

    5) Delays the process, if the other side is working against a deadline.

    6) Characterizes each change in his or her position as a major concession.

- A **cooperative negotiator** focuses on finding a mutually acceptable resolution, a win-win outcome. He or she uses the following strategies:

  1) Searches for ways to meet each party's *goals* and *interests*.

  2) Proposes as many options for resolution as possible.

  3) Begins with a realistic opening position and avoids announcing a "bottom line."

  4) Shares information.

  5) Refrains from making threats.

A Word to the Wise Negotiator

It is usually advantageous to keep the dialogue going. Remember that you always have three choices:

1) Accept the other side's last offer.
2) Reject their last offer and let an arbitrator or a judge make the decision.
3) Come up with something new, another proposal.

So long as you remember the third option, you can prevent unnecessary deadlock. It is always possible to modify your last offer (or the other side's last offer) enough to call it a new alternative, and thus keep the negotiation alive and the pressure on your opponent to accept. It is the best and only way to save face at the moment of deadlock and still keep the negotiation alive.

Gerald R. Williams, Professor of Law

Fifty-Six:
Learning to Listen

- Chances are that you don't engage in active listening. Most people have learned only strategic listening, which involves waiting for the other person to make a mistake, while planning a rebuttal. By contrast, active listening requires that you to try to understand the other person's perspective.

- One useful way to listen is to view the issues under discussion from the other person's point of view. Instead of listening for whether you agree or disagree, listen only for the *message*. Don't judge the content. Don't argue.

- You can practice active listening on the job or at home. When someone makes a statement, listen for the feeling. Are they angry, frustrated, hurt? Then listen for the content and paraphrase what you heard, stating both the feeling and the content, without adding an editorial comment, asking a question, or offering a solution. Example: "You are angry because you feel that we fired you unfairly." An easy way to begin an active listening response is, "You feel..."

- Active listening will boost your negotiating success. Understanding the conflict from the other side's perspective will enhance your chances of reaching an agreement that meets their needs, as well as your own. When the other side believes that you have understood their beliefs and feelings regarding the dispute, a shift occurs, making resolution more likely.

A New Way of Listening

Deborah and Jason began their divorce mediation session with arms crossed, facing away from each other. Once the preliminaries were over, I asked each of them to tell why they had come to mediation, suggesting that they listen with the goal of discovering one new thing about the other that they had not known before.

That session continued, others followed, and eventually the couple's divorce was finalized. Months later, I ran into the them, walking together with their young son, obviously enjoying each other's company. They told me that the skill they had learned in mediation--listening to discover--had had a profound impact on their lives. They felt less defensive and attacked when the other spoke, and recognized that, in spite of their differences, they still valued each other's friendship.

Samuel G. Mahaffy, Mediator

Fifty-Seven:
Trusting the Mediator

- One of the mediator's tasks is to help both sides come up with new solutions to their dispute. The more the mediator knows about the parties' underlying needs, the more able the mediator will be to help both sides find options that will work for them.

- In most mediations, each side will spend some time meeting with the mediator alone. Because these "caucuses" are confidential, the mediator is not permitted to share information with the other side, unless specifically authorized by the participants to do so.

- As a participant in a mediation, you should speak as candidly as possible with the mediator. Tell the mediator what you really want or need out of the mediation, and keep him or her abreast of changes in your thinking as the mediation progresses.

- One aspect of the mediator's job is to help you convey your needs to the other side and to help you evaluate each of the proposals that the other side makes for settlement. The more open you are in your communication with the mediator, the more able he or she will be to assist you.

- Keep in mind that the mediator is not a judge, but rather an aide in your effort to put this dispute behind you. Revealing weak or negative aspects of your role in the dispute to the mediator should not jeopardize your chances of reaching a satisfactory settlement, but rather enhance them.

Based on a survey done in 1993
by the American Bar Association,
the American public
takes a dim view of lawyers:

Only 26% view lawyers
as settlers of disputes.

Only 31% view lawyers
as problem solvers.

59% believe lawyers are greedy.

64% do *not* view lawyers
as seekers of justice.

Fifty-Eight:
Looking for Ways to Meet the Needs of Both Sides

- The ability of the parties and the mediator to think of solutions that will meet the needs of both sides is one of the keys to effective mediation. Mediation works best when the participants are willing to discard assumptions about how best to resolve a particular dispute and consider new possibilities.

- As a participant, you can optimize your chances of succeeding in mediation by inventing solutions that will benefit both you and the other side. Be creative. Make a long list of possibilities, including any ideas that come to mind. Don't evaluate or criticize any option, until all possibilities have been listed. Then look for individual items, or combinations, that might work. Look at each option and ask yourself, "Could this solution meet some or all of my needs?"

- Often both parties are too deeply mired in their anger and frustration to consider objectively the benefits of a proposed plan. When that happens, the mediator helps them express their feelings, so that they can evaluate their interests from a less emotional point of view. Once emotional barriers have been removed, the mediator can assist the participants in examining the pros and cons of each proposal.

- Often caucuses are needed in order to evaluate fully the ideas that are generated by brainstorming. After brainstorming in a joint session, you can request a caucus in order to discuss privately the solutions that have been proposed.

Severing the Ties that Bind

Rod and Lisa had been married for 22 years at the time of their divorce mediation. The laws of their state entitled Lisa to receive lifetime spousal support from Rod, a prospect which he abhorred. The couple had two adult sons. Their son Larry lived in a drug rehabilitation facility and was not legally entitled to any child support. Lisa hated the thought that Rod might not continue to support Larry until he completed treatment and became financially self-sufficient.

During their mediation, Rod identified his major goal as limiting his spousal support payments, and Lisa identified her major goal as insuring that Rod would continue to support Larry, both emotionally and financially .

After lengthy discussions, Rod agreed to attend family conferences at the drug rehabilitation center and to contribute substantially to Larry's financial support, until Larry got a job. Lisa agreed to terminate spousal support after one year of payments, waiving her right to an open-ended support order. Both were satisfied that their most important needs were met.

Jeanice Gross, MFCC & Mediator
Michael Gross, Attorney & Mediator

Fifty-Nine:
Creating a "High-Low Exchange"

- Often there is a special type of exchange between disputants which clinches a settlement. It occurs when one side agrees to give something to the other that is of *low cost* to the giver and *high value* to the recipient.

- The "high-low exchange" can take many forms. A person with more time than money may offer to perform a needed service, instead of compensating the other side financially. Alternatively, one side can offer an item of value that it doesn't need or can afford to give away to the other side, in lieu of making a cash payment.

- Words make good high-low exchanges. They are often experienced by the recipient as having high value. When one person voices appreciation or apologizes to another, a shift occurs. That shift allows the listener to consider possibilities for settling the dispute that seemed unthinkable before. Words of appreciation or apology can take the place of thousands of dollars.

- The participants, as well as the mediator, should watch for opportunities to create "high-low exchanges." They form part of the magic of mediation, and can infuse a seemingly hopeless dispute with new possibilities.

- Words of appreciation or apology create a high-low exchange only when uttered sincerely. Any attempt to trade words for money when the words are not spoken in truth is transparent and futile.

Grandfather's Pocket Watch

During their mediation, Ron and Maggie were discussing which household and personal items each would get in their divorce. Maggie paused and said softly, "... and there's my grandfather's pocket watch." Ron replied that Maggie had given him the watch as an anniversary present, and that it was legally his separate property.

Maggie began to talk about how much the watch meant to her, as one of only a few family treasures which had survived a fire years ago. Ron also spoke of how much he cared about the watch. Then he paused, and, after a moment of silence, offered to exchange the watch for the use of the garage, so that he would have a place to keep his things until he moved into a place of his own. Maggie agreed, because she had room in the garage, and the watch meant the world to her.

Jennifer Kresge, MFCC and Mediator

Sixty:
When to Settle and When to Walk

- "B.A.T.N.A." stands for your *best alternative to a negotiated agreement*.

- *Never* leave the mediation table without an agreement, unless you have carefully and unemotionally evaluated your B.A.T.N.A. and determined that you are willing and able to pay the price for rejecting the other side's last offer. Get some help in evaluating your alternatives to settlement. If you are personally involved in a dispute, you are probably not able to get enough distance from it to weigh your choices with a cool, clear head.

- View each offer of settlement strictly as a *business proposition*. You want to gain as much, or lose as little, as you possibly can. Only crusaders forego settlement for combat in order to pursue the *principle of the matter*. If you hear yourself saying, "It's the principle that counts!" take a break and cool off, before you give up a valuable opportunity to put your dispute behind you.

- Prioritize your needs ahead of time, then work hardest on meeting those at the top of your list.

- Gather enough information to be able to make a decision during the mediation about whether or not to accept a settlement offer. Evaluate as objectively as possible your chances of getting *everything* that you want, *some* of what you want, or (it can happen) *none* of what you want, in an arbitration or trial.

- What are your probable costs of pursuing justice by means of arbitration? Can you handle the preparation and presentation of your case yourself? If not, how much will it cost to pay a lawyer to represent you? What costs in time, money, and stress will you pay if you go to arbitration, with or without an attorney? If the arbitration is non-binding and your case goes to trial following the arbitration, what will that cost?

When Settlement Would Have Been Smart

Huerta v. Josephs
Defendant's offer	$ 500,000
Plaintiff's demand	$7,000,000
Verdict at trial	$ 0

McElroy v. Firestone
Defendant's offer	$1,000,000
Plaintiff's demand	$4,000,000
Verdict at trial	$ 0

King v. Square D
Defendant's offer	$ 125,000
Verdict at trial	$ 25,000

Rodriguez v. City of Visalia
Defendant's offer	$ 65,000
Verdict at trial	$ 11,500

Phillip J. Hermann, Attorney

Sixty-One:
How A Lawyer Can Help

- Look for a lawyer who understands that your goal is to reach a settlement, one who will assist you in putting your dispute behind you quickly and inexpensively.

- Interview at least two or three lawyers, before selecting one with whom you feel comfortable.

- Ask each lawyer to describe his or her training and experience in assisting clients in mediations.

- Ask for a written estimate of the cost of handling your case in mediation, in arbitration, and, if necessary, in court. Don't be afraid to discuss possible alternative fee arrangements.

- Ask each lawyer to tell you what the best arguments would be if he or she were the attorney on the other side. Knowing the weaknesses in your case can be as valuable as knowing the strengths.

- The attorney that you select can serve several functions, including conveying your legal rights clearly to the other side and to the mediator. Choose one who seems articulate and personable.

- Your lawyer should come up with options for resolving the conflict. During the mediation, he or she should help you decide whether to accept an offer of settlement or to reject it and continue negotiating. Although the final decision rests with you, your lawyer can provide a valuable service by pointing out the advantages and disadvantages of each offer.

"Although part of the impetus for increased ADR [alternative dispute resolution] is caused by the congested courts, a more powerful force is that many clients and an increasing number of lawyers are convinced that if a court precedent is not needed and there is no other need for a court judgment, an appropriate ADR process is often the better forum in which to resolve the dispute."

Robert D. Raven, Attorney
Past President, American Bar Association

Section 6 -- *CHOOSING THE RIGHT MEDIATOR FOR THE JOB*

Sixty-Two:
The "Muscle Mediators"

- "Muscle mediators" routinely offer their *opinion* of the appropriate settlement value of a case. Consequently, if you are looking for a mediator who will make a recommendation, you should choose a muscle mediator, one who will exercise his or her influence by applying pressure to settle quickly and predicting the outcome of your case in court.

- Most muscle mediators are attorneys or retired judges. Their mediations resemble settlement conferences, which are pretrial meetings between attorneys and judges, where settlement options are discussed and the odds of winning or losing at trial are assessed by both sides. Muscle mediators deal primarily with the attorneys, while the parties usually remain in the background.

- Muscle mediators aim for settlements that track with their view of the law, rather than searching for creative solutions to a dispute. They are inclined to impose their view of the best outcome.

- Because muscle mediators press hard for settlement, their mediations often take only one session. If you choose this type of mediator, wait a few minutes, or a few days, to consider the consequences of any proposed settlement agreement, *before* you sign it.

The Traits of a Good Mediator

1. The patience of Job
2. The sincerity and bulldog characteristics of the English
3. The wit of the Irish
4. The physical endurance of the marathon runner
5. The broken-field dodging abilities of a halfback
6. The guile of Machiavelli
7. The personality-probing skills of a good psychiatrist
8. The confidence-retaining characteristics of a mute
9. The hide of a rhinoceros
10. The wisdom of Solomon

William E. Simkin
Mediation and the Dynamics of Collective Bargaining

Sixty-Three:
The "Purists"

- The "purists" believe that their job is to *facilitate* the negotiations between the parties, *not* to offer their own opinions or press for a settlement. They won't tell you what they think the outcome of your case will be in court, nor will they give you any legal information or advice. They emphasize the *process*, rather than the end result.

- Purists believe that the resolution of a dispute should be driven primarily by the needs and interests of the parties, irrespective of the law. They encourage the disputants to express their *feelings* about the dispute, aiming for workable solutions, not legal perfection.

- If the purist approach appeals to you, the easiest way to locate a mediator who utilizes it is to call your nearest community dispute resolution center. You can also contact private mediators, to determine if they use this mediation model.

- Most purists call mediated agreements "memos," rather than "agreements" or "contracts." Regardless of the name, a signed document that sets forth the terms of a mediated agreement *is* binding upon all who sign it, except under unusual circumstances.

- Although some lawyers and judges have been trained in the purist model of mediation, purists are more likely to come from non-legal backgrounds. Many lawyers and judges are uncomfortable with the purist approach because they were trained to turn to the law for answers.

Sixty-Four:
The "Centrists"

- The "centrists" differ from the muscle mediators and the purists in several ways. Among other things, they generally will not offer their opinion of the outcome of your case in court, but will give you basic legal *information*. Unlike the purists, centrists often bring subject-matter expertise to the table.

- Centrists focus on the parties' needs, interests, and feelings, believing that most disputes have a strong emotional component that must be dealt with before a resolution on the factual issues can be reached.

- Because centrists believe that the disputants, not the attorneys, should take the lead, they encourage the disputants to do most of the talking. The attorneys function primarily in an advisory capacity.

- Like the purists, the centrists believe that people are more likely to comply with an agreement which they have negotiated directly. In order to facilitate negotiations between the parties, centrists may coach the participants in the use of communication techniques that will enhance their negotiating effectiveness. They often ask questions that will elicit the participants' underlying interests.

- Centrists generally encourage the disputants to take as much time as necessary to think about the consequences of their decisions. Because applying careful scrutiny to each issue tends to slow down the process, mediations handled by centrists often take *more* than one session to complete.

Differences Among Mediators

	Offer Opinions	Provide Legal Information	Apply Pressure to Settle	Predict Court Outcome	Encourage Negotiation Between the Parties	Encourage Expression of Feelings
Muscle Mediators	yes	always	yes	yes	no	no
Purists	no	never	no	no	yes	yes
Centrists	rarely	sometimes	no	rarely	yes	yes

Sixty-Five:
The Team Approach

- There's a lot of truth to the old adage, "two heads are better than one." That's why many mediators work in teams.

- Some of the most effective teams are made up of a lawyer and a psychotherapist.

- Many people feel more comfortable with a team that is comprised of both a man and a woman, particularly in family matters, such as divorce.

- A team of mediators can divide tasks. While one writes on a board, away from those at the mediation table, the other can interact more closely with the participants. While one helps the participants brainstorm for new solutions, the other can use a calculator to check the consequences of a particular proposal.

- During especially emotional times in a mediation, each team member can "caucus" with one side separately. This ability to hold simultaneous caucuses is particularly important when a dispute becomes volatile and the participants feel inclined to abandon the mediation.

- Although you may pay a higher hourly rate for a team of mediators than for a solo mediator, the increased effectiveness and efficiency of an experienced team generally warrant the higher price.

"The purpose of our civil justice system is to make victims whole, not rich."

Citizens Against Lawsuit Abuse

Sixty-Six:
Your Mediator's Qualifications

- Most states have set no requirements for mediators; however, some states and some courts require mediators who wish to receive court referrals to obtain approved mediation training, as well as to have mediation experience.

- The best way to choose a mediator is to get a referral from a friend or colleague who has experienced a successful mediation.

- Before you select a mediator, call a few and ask them to describe their training, experience, methods, and fees. A list of questions appears in Chapter 68. Your *overall response* to each mediator is more important than the answer to any one question. Does he or she sound professional? Is he or she a good listener?

- Check for conflicts of interest. If the person or company with whom you have a dispute suggests that you use a specific mediator, ask if they have ever had any relationship with that mediator. If a prior relationship exists, question the mediator's neutrality.

- Make sure that you get answers to all of your questions. Mediators respond to inquiries from potential clients in different ways. Some answer questions over the phone, others hold a free initial orientation session, and still others mail a brochure or videotape to prospective clients, describing themselves and their services.

*"There is a lot of diversity
of approach in the field,
and one of the things
we're beginning to see is
that there is not a single model
that works in all situations."*

James Boskey, Professor of Law

Sixty-Seven:
The Price Tag

- The cost of a mediation can vary all the way from nothing to thousands of dollars per day.

- Community dispute resolution centers often provide excellent mediation services, at little or no cost. If they use a sliding scale, however, you may pay as much as you would with a private mediator.

- Most private mediators charge by the hour, although some charge by the day. Since you can save hundreds or thousands of dollars in attorney's fees and other court costs if mediation is successful, base your selection on the mediator's ability and experience, not on the cost.

- Some mediators require payment in advance. When such is the case, ask for a written agreement which entitles you to recover any *unused* portion of the fee.

- Some mediators charge an administrative fee, in addition to their hourly fee. This may take the form of an amount per participant or a lump sum.

- Some mediators charge a flat fee. This has advantages and disadvantages. An advantage is that you will know the cost in advance. A disadvantage is that the mediator may pressure you to enter into a hasty settlement, in order to maximize his or her hourly income.

"Some litigators cannot conceive of handling a case without the usual overstaffing and overkill. Meanwhile, settlement negotiations must take place on the courthouse steps, after nearly all the potential fees have been earned and the litigator suddenly (and conveniently) recommends settlement."

John W. Toothman, Attorney

Sixty-Eight:
Ten Questions to Ask in Advance

You can use this list to ask mediators about their qualifications, policies, and procedures.

1) What is your background? What mediation training and experience have you had?

2) What is your experience with this type of case?

3) Do you practice team, or solo, mediation?

4) What is your fee structure?

5) Do you hold caucuses? If so, do you keep the information you obtain confidential?

6) What can we expect to happen in the sessions?

7) Will you continue to work toward settlement by phone, if this matter doesn't get resolved during the mediation sessions?

8) Will you prepare the final agreement and any other paperwork that is needed to resolve this dispute? Will you file it with the court?

9) Have you ever had any connections with the other side?

10) How many hours (or sessions) would you estimate will be necessary? How soon can we start?

"Every rational party to a dispute wants it to end."

Judge Frank B. Zinn, retired
Albuquerque, New Mexico

Sixty-Nine:
The Client's Bill of Rights

- You have the right to make fully-informed, completely voluntary, decisions.

- You have the right to take as much time as you need, in order to make decisions that will work for you in the long-run.

- You have the right to change your mind and renegotiate any issue, until you sign the final agreement.

- You have the right to leave mediation at any time, if the process is not working for you.

- You have the right to know the mediator's fees, before you begin.

- You have the right to be treated with respect, by the mediator, as well as the participants.

- You have the right to be assisted by a mediator who is neutral and uninvested in the outcome of your dispute, one who has no stake in the terms of your settlement or in whether or not your case settles.

- You have the right to get outside legal advice at any time during the mediation.

- You have the right, in a divorce mediation, to full disclosure from your spouse on all financial issues.

"When will I be old enough to start suing people?"

Section 7 -- *ARBITRATION: A USER'S GUIDE*

Seventy:
Arbitration -- A Quick, Cheap Substitute for a Trial

- Arbitration isn't really new. It's been used to resolve union-management disputes since the 1920's. For years, federal law has mandated arbitration in areas such as air traffic control and railroad transportation, where the public health and safety are at stake.

- Until recently, arbitration was a tool that was utilized primarily by government and big business. Today it is readily available to all of us.

- What is an arbitrator? An arbitrator is someone who acts as a judge. His or her job is to evaluate the evidence, determine who's right and who's wrong, make a decision, and render an award.

- When should you use arbitration? Use arbitration any time that you have tried mediation unsuccessfully, or have a good reason for not attempting mediation in the first place.

- You shouldn't use either mediation *or* arbitration when you want to make a change in the law by setting a legal precedent. To accomplish that, you will need to go through a trial and then win an appeal.

- If you feel that you need to tug at the heartstrings of a jury in order to secure a financial windfall, arbitration won't meet your needs either. You'll need a jury trial if you want to make a killing on your case.

- Should you involve an attorney? Even in the smallest case, a consultation with an attorney can be invaluable. If your case is complicated, or you don't have time to prepare it, you should hire an attorney to represent you at the arbitration.

- You can initiate an arbitration at any time, whether or not you've filed a lawsuit.

"One might envision by the year 2000 not simply a courthouse but a dispute resolution center, where the grievant would first be channeled through a screening clerk who would then direct him to the process, or sequence of processes, most appropriate to his type of case."

Frank E. A. Sander, Professor
Harvard Law School
Addressing the Pound Conference, 1976

Seventy-One:
Binding or Nonbinding?

- Arbitration can be either *binding* or *nonbinding*, depending upon the wishes of the parties. The ruling in a binding arbitration is final and usually cannot be appealed. After an unsatisfactory nonbinding arbitration, the loser can request a trial and take another shot at winning.

- When a court orders a case to arbitration, the decision of the arbitrator is generally *nonbinding*, unless the parties request otherwise. One disadvantage of participating in a nonbinding arbitration is that your opponent can use the process as a dress rehearsal, previewing your case, in order better to prepare for trial. Another disadvantage of nonbinding arbitration is that a shrewd opponent may reject the arbitrator's award, and then threaten to take the matter to trial, in order to gain additional leverage in negotiating a pretrial settlement.

- The advantage of binding arbitration is that both sides dispose of the dispute *for once and for all*. The risks and costs of further litigation are foreclosed.

- If the law is clearly on your side, or if putting the dispute behind you is a high priority, you should select *binding* arbitration, since your opponent will be precluded from prolonging the process by requesting a trial and, perhaps, later pursuing an appeal. However, if your case is shaky, or you want to preserve your right to a trial and later an appeal, if necessary, you should choose *nonbinding* arbitration, in order to keep your options open.

Arbitration

	Binding	Nonbinding
OK to do it yourself?	Yes.	Yes.
OK to use an attorney?	Yes.	Yes.
Arbitrator's award final?	Yes, with few exceptions.	No, either side may request a "trial de novo."
OK to bring witnesses?	Yes.	Yes.
Who selects the arbitrator?	Both sides agree.	Both sides agree.
Who pays?	Each party pays, unless a contract states that the loser pays.	Each party pays, unless a contract states that the loser pays.

Seventy-Two:
What Rules Will Apply?

- Commercial arbitration firms generally provide written rules which apply to the cases they handle. Often they apply different sets of rules to different types of cases. You can request a copy of the appropriate rules and then determine whether or not they are acceptable to you. The arbitration rules to which you agree should allow you to present all of the evidence that you consider important and to have reasonable access ahead of time to evidence gathered by the other side.

- One advantage of using arbitration instead of going through a trial in court is that you and your opponent can agree in advance on the rules to be applied to your case. These are generally less complicated than the court's rules of evidence, allowing you to introduce evidence that might otherwise be excluded, so long as the arbitrator views it as relevant.

- You can request that the arbitrator assist in establishing a schedule for the exchange of documents and a timetable for the exchange of information, such as lists of witnesses to be called at the hearing.

- You and the other side can streamline the process by agreeing in advance to give the arbitrator a written statement in which both sides "stipulate" to any uncontested facts. This saves time and money by narrowing the issues to be presented at the hearing to those which are contested.

*"I was ruined but twice in life,
once when I won a lawsuit,
and once when I lost one."*

Voltaire

Seventy-Three:
Is One Arbitrator Enough?

- For the same reason that you might prefer a jury composed of twelve people to a single judge, you might prefer a panel of three arbitrators to a single arbitrator.

- Because it's less expensive to hire a single arbitrator, the vast majority of cases that go to arbitration are handled that way. Although the main deterrent to using a panel is the cost, another drawback is the time it takes to schedule a hearing. Generally, you have to wait longer to convene an arbitration panel than you do to set a date for a single arbitrator to hear your case.

- If you decide to use a panel, you have some additional decisions to make ahead of time. Do you want the arbitrators to reach a *consensus* or to *average* their individual results? Do you want to throw out the low and the high decisions and accept the opinion of the arbitrator whose award is in the middle? Although the standard rules require a majority decision, you can request a variation that both you and the other side prefer.

- Complex cases involving a great deal of money are often best handled by a panel of arbitrators. The old adage "there's safety in numbers" applies here. You are less apt to get stuck with a decision that is way out of line, if you entrust your case to three people, rather than submitting it to a single arbitrator.

"We must develop and maintain the capacity to forgive. He who is devoid of the power to forgive, is devoid of the power to love."

Thoreau

Seventy-Four:
Your Arbitrator's Qualifications

- If you decide to submit your dispute to arbitration, you and your opponent will need to agree on an arbitrator (or panel of arbitrators). You have four choices: 1) you can contact a *company* that specializes in arbitration, 2) you can select an *attorney* who handles arbitrations, 3) you can use an *expert* in a field that is related to your dispute, or 4) you can choose *any person* that both sides trust to render a fair and impartial decision.

- Experienced arbitration companies have the advantage of having handled thousands of arbitrations. They employ administrators to coordinate schedules and handle other pre-hearing arrangements.

- Private attorneys who handle arbitrations may be able to save you money that you would otherwise have to pay to a larger organization for their administrative and room rental fees.

- Whether you choose an attorney or a non-attorney to act as your arbitrator, if your issues are technical, select someone with experience in the subject matter of your dispute, so that he or she can fully comprehend the factual issues and the jargon.

- Watch out for the arbitrator who has repeatedly handled cases for the other side. Request information about your arbitrator's rulings on cases similar to yours. Do his or her awards favor or disfavor similarly situated litigants?

Employees Beware

Employers who repeatedly use the same arbitrators have a much higher victory rate than do employers who do not make repeated use of an arbitrator.

Out of 232 claims brought by employees in non-union employment cases, the odds were 5 to 1 against the employee in repeat-player cases, whereas the odds were 2.4 to 1 in favor of the employee in nonrepeat-player cases.

Lisa Bingham, University of Indiana

Seventy-Five:
Estimating Costs

- Arbitrators' fees are relatively modest, especially when compared to the cost of a trial. The largest part of your cost for an arbitration will be your attorney's fees, if you decide you don't want to handle the job by yourself.

- Many arbitrators charge an administrative fee for setting up the hearing, as well as an hourly fee. Find out whether the administrative fee, and any other fees that you are required to pay in advance, are refundable, in part or in whole, in the event that the arbitration is cancelled. Also find out when the hourly fee is due and how many hours the arbitrator estimates will be needed to complete your case.

- Ask whether or not the arbitrator charges for reading paperwork that you or the other side submit in advance. Will you be charged for phone calls? For time spent in writing up the award? For the rental of an office in which to hold the hearing? Who pays?

- Once you have estimated the number of hours that the arbitration is likely to take, multiply that number by the hourly fee and add the administrative fee, as well as any other costs, such as attorney and expert witnesses fees, and exhibit preparation expenses. If the figure seems high, remind yourself of your reasons for choosing this short-cut. You will save time, money, heartaches, and headaches by bringing an end to your dispute quickly and getting on with more pleasant and profitable pursuits.

Final Thoughts

- *Although mediation can be difficult, most people have the ability to connect with each other and to resolve their own problems, given the opportunity to do so.*

- *Family matters should rarely, if ever, be decided in court.*

- *Mediation should be a mandatory first step in every dispute, a step to be taken before any lawsuit is filed. Reserve court as a last resort, using it only in those rare instances where the dispute can't be resolved more peacefully.*

- *Each of us has too few days on earth to waste (m)any of them embroiled in a dispute.*

Acknowledgements

Page 11: Robert A. Baruch Bush, Professor, Hofstra University School of Law, Hempstead, New York. Reprinted with permission of the National Institute for Dispute Resolution Forum.

Page 17: ABA Journal, September 1993, *VOX POPULI, The Public Perception of Lawyers: ABA Poll*, by Gary A. Hengstler, © 1993 American Bar Association. Reprinted by permission of the ABA Journal.

Page 21: Sue Grafton, **"K" is for Killer**, © 1994 by Sue Grafton, reprinted by permission of Henry Holt and Co., Inc.

Page 23: Sam Benson, Attorney, Colorado Springs, Colorado.

Page 25: Michael J. Roberts, Attorney, Mediator, and Arbitrator San Diego, California.

Page 29: Betty McManus, Public Relations Coordinator, San Diego Dispute Resolution Center, San Diego, California.

Page 31: Judith Filner, Attorney, National Institute for Dispute Resolution, ABA Journal, August 1996, *The Lawyer Turns Peacemaker*, by Richard C. Reuben, © 1996 American Bar Association. Reprinted by permission of the ABA Journal.

Page 37: A. David Puzo, Attorney, Carlsbad, California.

Page 47: Center for Public Resources, Institute for Dispute Resolution, New York, New York.

Page 51: American Bar Association, *Facts About the American Civil Justice System*.

Page 53: Citizens Against Lawsuit Abuse, Torrance, California.

Page 63: Frank E. A. Sander, Professor, Harvard Law School, ABA Journal, August 1996, *The Lawyer Turns Peacemaker,* by Richard C. Reuben, © 1996 American Bar Association. Reprinted by permission of the ABA Journal.

Page 71: Mary Mudd Quinn, Ph. D., MFCC, and Mediator; J. William Hargreaves, Attorney and Mediator, San Diego, California.

Page 75: Sandra Day O'Conner, Justice U.S. Supreme Court. Reprinted from the Texas Bar Journal, January 1988.

Page 77: Robert E. Adler. Reprinted from *Divorce--133 Ways to Diffuse the Battle--A New Approach,* by Forrest S. Bayard.

Page 79: *The Lawyer Turns Peacemaker,* by Richard C. Reuben, ABA Journal, August 1996. © 1996 American Bar Association. Reprinted by permission of the ABA Journal.

Page 93: Herman Wacker, Attorney, Seattle, Washington.

Page 97: Nancy Neal Yeend, from *Dispute Resolution for Small Businesses,* ADR Applications, Inc., Senior Vice President Systems Design, St. Petersburg, Florida.

Page 98: Partnering: Nancy Neal Yeend, from *Dispute Resolution for Small Businesses,* ADR Applications, Inc., Senior Vice President-Systems Design, St. Petersburg, Florida.

Page 103: Michael D. Shook and Jeffrey D. Meyer, *Legal Briefs,* Macmillan, © 1995.

Page 105: Liz O'Brien, President, San Diego Mediation Center, San Diego, California.

Page 107: Michael Schulte, Attorney, Sacramento, California. California Bar Journal September 1996, by permission of the California Bar Journal.

Page 117: Andrew Magolin, Clinical Psychologist, Mansfield, Massachusetts.

Page 119: Gerald R. Williams, Professor of Law, Brigham Young University, Provo, Utah.

Page 121: Samuel G. Mahaffy, Mediator, Spokane, Washington.

Page 124: ABA Journal, September 1993, *VOX POPULI, The Public Perception of Lawyers: ABA Poll,* by Gary A. Hengstler, © 1993 American Bar Association. Reprinted by permission of the ABA Journal.

Thank You

We want to thank the following people who so generously gave of their time to assist us with their ideas about the writing and publishing of this book. Their efforts helped shape it in many ways.

Pat Stein, David Kelly, J.D., Andrea Adams Kelly, M.S., Mary Mudd Quinn, Ph.D., Jeanice Gross, M.A., Michael Gross, J.D., Betty McManus, J.D., Louis Storrow, J.D., Mari Frank, J.D., Leslie Lindquist, M.B.A., Professor Nancy Rogers, J.D., Jennifer Kresge, M.A., Alan Kellock, Jyl Steinback, Martin Ashley, J.D., Deborah Fay, M.A., Gregory W. McBain, P.E., Rebecca Grudemeyer, Psy.D., David Grudemeyer, Ph.D., Dennis Sharp, J.D., Professor Gerald R. Williams, J.D., Terry Elliot McShane, M.A., Scott Mather, Val Bright, Vicki Green, J.D., Eileen M. Meuris, Ed.D., and Donald Webb, Ph.D.

We also want to thank the following staff members who worked tirelessly on our book's production.

Constance Miller, Candice Loertcher, Angelka Curcic, and Stacy Krahl.

DIRECTORY OF REFERRAL SOURCES

The following listings include organizations which can refer you to mediators and/or arbitrators. The authors have attempted to include a representative sampling. Neither the authors nor the publisher endorse any particular organization.

Academy of Family Mediators
4 Militia Drive
Lexington, MA 02173
Tel: (617) 674-2663
Fax: (617) 674-2690

Association of Family and
Conciliation Courts
329 W. Wilson Street
Madison, WI 53703
Tel: (608) 251-4001
Fax: (608) 251-2231

National Association for
Community Mediation
1726 "M" St. NW Ste. 500
Washington, D.C. 20036-4502
Tel: (202) 467-6226 EXT 3
Fax: (202) 466-4769
Member Directory: $35.00

Family Firm Institute
Lenny Fogel
12 Harris Street
Brookline, MA 02146
Tel: (617) 738-1591
Fax: (617) 738-4883

Council of Better
Business Bureaus
4200 Wilson Blvd, 8th Floor
Arlington, VA 22203-1804
Tel: (703) 276-0100
Fax: (703) 276-0634

International Alliance of
Holistic Lawyers
Bill van Zyverden
P.O Box 753
Middlebury, VT 05753
Tel: (802) 388-7478

Conflict Resolution Center
International
Paul Wahrhaftig
2205 E. Carson Street
Pittsburgh, PA 15203-2107
Tel: (412) 481-5559
Fax: (412) 481-5601
E-Mail: crci@igc.apc.org
Membership Directory: $150.00

DIRECTORY OF PROVIDERS WITH OFFICES IN SEVERAL CITIES

The following listings include those providers of mediation and arbitration services that have offices in several cities. Contact this office for information regarding their other locations. Neither the authors nor the publisher endorse any particular provider.

Codes indicate areas of practice: **CA**= Commercial arbitration and **CM**= Commercial mediation (which includes a wide variety of categories).

American Arbitration Association
AAA Center for Med.   CA CM
140 W. 51st. Street
New York, NY 10020
Tel: (212)484-4000

Florida Med. Group   CA CM
A. Nicholson/Burt Lowlicht F S N
28 W. Flager St. Ste. 1010
Miami, FL 33130
Tel: (305) 579-9990
Fax: (305) 579-9991
E-Mail: fmg@2mediate.com

JAMS Endispute   CM
1920 Main Street Ste. 300
Irvine, CA 92714
Tel: (714) 224-1810
Fax: (714) 224-1819

Judicate West   CA CM
Alternative Dispute Res. Center
1851 E. First St. Ste. 1450
Santa Ana, CA 92705
Tel: (800) 488-8805
Fax: (714) 834-1344

Legal Gard   CA CM
123 Chestnut Ste. 401
Philadelphia, PA 19106
Tel: (215) 923-4200
Fax: (215) 923-4223

Resolute Systems   CA CM
16655 W. Bluemound Road
Brookfield, WI 53008
Tel: (800) 359-4222

U. S. Arb. & Mediation   CA CM
3637 Markham Drive
Bensalem, PA 19020
Tel: (800) 354-2478

DIRECTORY OF PROVIDERS

The authors have attempted to include a representative sampling of mediators and arbitrators; however, because of space limitations, many providers could not be included. Neither the authors nor the publisher endorse or recommend any particular provider.

Codes indicate areas of practice: **CA**= Commercial arbitration, **CM**= Commercial mediation (which includes a wide variety of categories) **F**= Family mediation **S**= School mediation, **N**= Neighborhood mediation, and **PF**= Publicly funded.

If you do not find a provider near you:

• Call the National Institute for Dispute Resolution (NIDR) at (202) 466-4764 for a referral to a statewide association.
• Ask a therapist, a lawyer, or a judge for a referral.
• Check your Yellow Pages under "Mediation" or "Arbitration."

ALABAMA
Alabama Divorce Mediation
Lee Borden   F
3280 Morgan Drive
Birmingham, AL 35216
Tel: (205) 979-6960
Fax: (205) 979-6902

Janzen, Gayle S.   F
2 Riverchase Ofc Plaza Ste. 115
Birmingham, AL 35244
Tel: (205) 403-0955
Fax: (205) 403-0956

Kramer, Luther E.   F
219 Grove Ave
Huntsville, AL 35801
Tel: (205) 534-2560
Fax: (205) 536-5508

Kok, Sammye Oden   F
2121 Highland Avenue
Birmingham, AL 35205
Tel: (205) 939-0033
Fax: (205) 933-6133

ALASKA
AK Associates
Frank Gold   F
3098 Airport Way
Faribanks, AK 99709
Tel: (907) 474-9292
Fax: (907) 455-4369
E-Mail: akgold@alaska,net

Arbitration & Mediation Group
Kathleen G. Anderson   F
P.O. Box 240783
Anchorage, AK 99524
Tel: (907) 345-3801
Fax: (907) 345-0006

Cravez, Glenn   CA CM F N
421 West First Avenue Ste. 250
Anchorage, AK 99501
Tel: (907) 276-3370
Fax: (907) 276-8238

Dearborn Family Mediation
Mary Ann Dearborn   F
308 G Street #202
Anchorage, AK 99501
Tel: (907) 276-6001

Lazur & Luzur, Ltd.
Louise & Richard Lazur   F
741 Sesame Street
Anchorage, AK 99503-6641
Tel: (907) 562-1933
Fax: (907) 562-1931

Peninsula Mediation
Sara Louise Jackinsky   F
Box 1044
Homer, AK 99603
Tel: (907) 235-6417
Fax: (907) 235-1045

Peterson, Drew   F
4325 Laurel #235
Anchorage, AK 99508
Tel: (907) 561-1518
Fax: (907) 562-0780

Scott, Susan R.   F
10941 Kaskanak Drive
Eagle River, AK 99577
Tel: (907) 696-0862

Sullivan-Batra, Lorraine   F
27345 Golden Eagle Drive
Chugiak, AK 99567
Tel: (907) 279-3695
Fax: (907) 258-2157

ARKANSAS
Crigler & Associates
P.W. Crigler   F S N
101 Emporia Street
Eureka Springs, AR 72632
Tel: (501) 253-4999
Fax: (501) 253-4999
E-Mail: pwcrigler@aol.com

ARIZONA
Accord Mediation Services
Linda Devoy   F
177 North Church Ave. Ste. 200
Tucson, AZ 85701-1117
Tel: (602) 628-7777
Fax: (602) 623-5074

Arriola, Shannon R.   F
10900 N. Scottsdale Rd. Ste. 201
Scottsdale, AZ 85254
Tel: (602) 596-1226
Fax: (602) 948-8163

Borum, Joy   F
7520 East 2nd Street #3
Scottsdale, AZ 85251
Tel: (602) 945-8909
Fax: (602) 9452650

Capra, Shari   F
340 East Palm Lane Ste. 275
Phoenix, AZ 85004
Tel: (602) 271-4244
Fax: (602) 271-9308

Crabb, Jimmy   F
3010 East Loretta Drive
Tucson, AZ 85716-2527
Tel: (602) 323-1801
Fax: (602) 323-1801

Dispute Management Resources
Kim McCandless   CM F S N
10185 E. Larkspur Drive
Scottsdale, AZ 85260
Tel: (602) 661-6398
Fax: (602) 661-6000

Divorce & Family Mediation
Suzanna A. Norbeck   F
1807 E. Hale
Mesa, AZ 85203
Tel: (602) 649-9970

Divorce Mediation Center
Linda Brewster/Gordon Giles F
7520 E. Second Street Ste. 7
Scottsdale, AZ 85251
Tel: (602) 994-8787
Fax: (602) 941-2650

Family Mediation Center
Allison H. Quattrocchi   F
7520 E. 2nd Street #3
Scottsdale, AZ 85251
Tel: (602) 949-9511
Fax: (602) 941-2650

Fine, Tobe   CM, F, N
6056 North Tocito Place
Tucson, AZ 85718
Tel: (520) 577-0444

Gourley, Ruth L.   F
1703 South Cholla Avenue
Mesa, AZ 85202
Tel: (602) 506-2300
Fax: (602) 506-2029

Kuzma, Zenia   F
114 North San Francisco #205
Flagstaff, AZ 86001
Tel: (602) 774-8423

Lane, Pamela S.   F
8636 East Jumping Cholla Circle
Gold Canyon, AZ 85219
Tel: (602) 982-1388

LaVelle, Margaret E.   F
4524 North 13th Avenue
Phoenix, AZ 85013
Tel: (602) 264-7601

Lee, S. Terry   F
10220 North 31st Ave. Ste. 225
Phoenix, AZ 85051
Tel: (602) 870-9700
Fax: (602) 870-9783

Lifeskills Program Services, Inc.
Jerilyn L. Evans-Graff   F
2222 S. Dobson Rd. Ste. 802
Mesa, AZ 85202
Tel: (602) 967-0665
Fax: (602) 820-2441
Jerilyn-Evans-Graff@msn.cont.

Moore, John P.   F
394 N. 3rd Ave
Phoenix, AZ 85003
Tel: (602) 258-3400
Fax: (602) 258-7557

Musty, Timothy A.   F
2200 E. River Rd. Ste. 118A
Tucson, AZ 85718-6579
Tel: (520) 577-0079
Fax: (520) 577-0169

Nicholson, Ford T.   F
3912 S. Lone Palm Dr.
Tuscon, AZ 85730
Tel: (602) 740-5590
Fax: (602) 624-4034

Orman, Betty   F
5262 N. Adobe Circle
Tucson, AZ 85750
Tel: (520) 795-0300
Fax: (520) 747-3912

Our Town   PF
3830 E. Bellvue   CM S N
Tucson, AZ 85716
Tel: (520) 323-1708

Out-of-Court Solutions
Oliver Ross   CM F
3420 Shea Blvd. Ste. 216
Phoenix, AZ 85028
Tel: (602) 953-5216
Fax: (602) 953-5316
E-Mail: mediate@primenet.com

Remers, Ann Jordan   F
5022 E. Calle Guebabi
Tucson, AZ 85718
Tel: (502) 529-8610
Fax: (502) 529-8610

Richter, Kay   F
1790 E. River Rd.
Tucson, AZ 85718
Tel: (602) 577-5275

Rieder, Katherine   CM F N
711 S. Granite St. Ste. D
Prescott, AZ 86303
Tel: (520) 772-5156

Robb, Karen   F
201 W. Jefferson
Phownix, AZ 85003
Tel: (602) 506-3296

Scottsdale Counseling & Med.
Kathleen D. Infeld/Marlen Joy F
10900 N. Scottsdale Rd. Ste. 501
Scottsdale, AZ 85254
Tel: (602) 948-2635
Fax: (602) 948-8163

Tobin, Joan F.   F
2171 E. La Donna Drive
Tempe, AZ 85283
Tel: (602) 839-8992

CALIFORNIA

Accord Mediation
J.R. Hastings & Judith Parker F
18 San Rafael Avenue
San Anselmo, CA 94960
Tel: (800) 358-2152
Fax: (415) 459-6756

Action Dispute Resolution Svc
Lucie Barron   CA CM F
11755 Wilshire Blvd., Ste. 1400
Los Angeles, CA 90025-1520
Tel: (310) 444-1435
Fax: (310) 444-1406

Adams, Nancy A.   F
550 N. State Street Ste. 4
Ukiah, CA 95482
Tel: (707) 468-7871
Fax: (707) 467-0121

Aden, Melvin O.   CM N
348 Windjammer Circle
Chula Vista, CA 91910
Tel: (619) 427-4022
Fax; (619) 427-4022

Airola, Kay   F
675 Jefferson St. #6
Monterey, CA 93940
Tel: (408) 375-0547
E-Mail: Kayairola.aol.com

Alkire, Marie Comstock   F
3579 Arlington Avenue Ste. 300
Riverside, CA 92506
Tel: (909) 369-5260
Fax: (909) 369-5003

Alliance Mediation Services
Michael G. Pipich   F
100 S. Citrus Ave #206
Covina, CA 91723
Tel: (818) 915-7581
Fax: (818) 915-7588
E-Mail: Mpipich1@aol.com

Alternative Legal Solutions
Ron Perring   F CM
647 W. Shaw Suite 1
Fresno, CA 93704
Tel: (209) 226-4327
Fax: (209) 229-0630
E-Mail: perring@cybgete.com

Alternatives - A Mediation Svc
Laurelle Thom   F
43 Quail Cout Suite 211
Walnut Creek, CA 94596
Tel: (510) 930-9446
Fax: (510) 930-0911

Alternatives: Divorce Mediation
Debrorah A. Vaupen   F
1421 Santa Monica Blvd Ste 101
Santa Monica, CA 90404
Tel: (310) 587-0077
Fax: (310) 587-3330
E-Mail: divmediate@aol.com

American Ass'n for Med. Div.
Richard & Marilyn Ruman   F
211 S. Beverly Dr., Ste. 109
Beverly Hills, CA 90212
Tel: (310) 247-1920
Fax: (310) 247-9661

Angel-Levy, Penny   F
5060 Shoreham Place, Ste. 200
San Diego, CA 92122
Tel: (619) 458-5878

Baker-Jackson, Maxine   F
7504 Via Lorado
Rancho Palos Verdes, CA 90275
Tel: (310) 377-5311

Bardin, Carole   F
23842 Bothina Bay
Dana Point, CA 92629
Tel: (714) 454-6314
Fax: (310) 692-3431

Batchelder, Hadley   CA CM F
2121 San Diego Avenue
San Diego, CA 92110-2986
Tel: (619) 297-9700
Fax; (619) 294-4713
E-Mail: hadleyb@TJSL.edu

Better Solutions Mediation Svc.
Janis Weaver   CM F N
17671 Irvine Blvd, Ste. 120
Tustin, CA 92780
Tel: (714) 637-9142
Fax: (714) 637-0134

Blaettler, John   F
7881 Church Street Ste. B
Gilroy, CA 95020
Tel: (408) 848-2730
Fax: (408) 848-5356

Brand, Norman   CA CM
156 Lombard Street #22
San Francisco, CA 94111
Tel: (415) 982-7172
Fax: (415) 982-8021

Bricker , Gary   CA CM S N
2222 Francisco Dr. #430
El Dorado Hills, CA 95762
Tel: (916) 939-4299
Fax: (916) 939-0250

Brown, Brad   CA CM F
4401 Manchester Ave. Ste 706
Encinitas, CA 92024-4939
Tel: (619) 753-0783

California Mediation Center
Joan B. Kelly   F
100 Tamal Plaza Ste. 175
Corte Madera, CA 94925
Tel: (415) 927-1422
Fax: (415) 927-1477

California Mediation Group
Lori Riffice   F
2140 Professional Drive Ste. 200
Roseville, CA 95661
Tel: (916) 782-4033
Fax: (916) 782-4033

Castrey, Bonnie   CM F
P.O. Box 5007
Huntington Beach, CA 92615
Tel: (714) 963-7114
Fax: (714) 964-2495

Center for ADR
David E. Hayen   CA CM
1223 Wilshire Blvd., Ste. 816
Santa Monica, CA 90403
Tel: (310) 202-6324
Fax: (310) 202-6397

Center for Dispute Resolution
Kenneth Cloke   F
2411 18th Street
Santa Monica, CA 90405
Tel: (310) 399-4426
Fax: (310) 399-5906

Centerpoint Mediation   F
Frances Hayward/N. McGovern
19762 MacArthur Blvd.
Irvine, CA 92612
Tel: (714) 495-4700
Fax: (714) 495-1731

Coast to Coast Med. Ctr   CM F
Elizabeth Allen/Don Mohr
4401 Manchester Ave. Ste 202
Encinitas, CA 92024
Tel: (800) 748-6462
Fax: (619) 436-7943
E-Mail: staff@ctcmediation.com

Cohen, Renee   F
3480 Torrance Blvd.
Torrance, CA 90503
Tel: (310) 541-9978
Fax: (310) 541-9978

Creating Solutions
Gretchen A. Brambach   CM F
232 San Antonio Way
Walnut Creek, CA 94598
Tel: (510) 934-2083

Dispute Resolution Specialists
R. Michael Kasperzak CA CM N
1172 Morton Court
Mountain View, CA 94040
Tel: (415) 948-5340
Fax; (415) 948-5076
mkasperzak@mediates.com

Divorce Helpline
Anne Lober   F
2425 Porter St Ste. 18
Soquel, CA 95073
Tel: (408) 464-1114
Fax: (408) 464-0509
E-Mail: wbox@divorcehelp.com

170

Divorce & Family Med. Svc.
Doris Figman/Julie Morris   F
653 11th St.
Oakland, CA 94607
Tel: (510) 465-6518
Fax: (510) 465-1566

Douthit, Zona/Tobin, Thomas F
23 Altarinda Ste. 206
Orinda, CA 94563
Tel: (510) 253-3111

Eddy, William   F
160 Thorn Street Ste. 2
San Diego, CA 92103-5657
Tel: (619) 291-9644
Fax: (619) 692-4061

Equitable Mediation Services
Earle Warner   CA CM F S N
22047 Canyon Drive
Wildomar, CA 92595
Tel: (909) 983-0111
Tel: (909) 245-2106

Fair Ways Mediation Center
Edward J. Pallotta, Jr.   F
301 Forest Ave.
Laguna Beach, CA 92651
Tel: (714) 494-6068
Fax: (714) 494-8318
discovered@aol.com

Family Law Assistance
Joan McKillican   F
10391 Friars Road Ste. B
San Diego, CA 92120
Tel: (619) 280-5444
Fax: (619) 280-5546

Family Law Mediation Ctr.
Rhonda Rauch & Ellen Tinero F
Michael Greenwald
15915 Ventura Blvd Ste. 203
Encino, CA 91436
Tel: (818) 986-4568
Fax: (818) 995-8363

Family Preservation Med. Svc.
Joseph Meyer & Nellie Pedro F
1131 S. Rexford Drive Ste. 3
Los Angeles, CA 90035
Tel: (310) 726-9414

Family Mediation Center
Kenneth M. Blonsley   F
1308 Main St. Ste. 103
St. Helena, CA 94574
Tel: (707) 963-3161

Family Mediation Service
Donald T. Saposnek   F
6233 Soquel Dr. Ste. E
Aptos, CA 95003
Tel: (408) 476-9225
Fax: (408) 662-9056

Farnaes, Annette   CM F N
5383 Bothe Ave
San Diego, CA 92122
Tel: (619) 546-1024
E-Mail: farnaes@aol.com

Feldman-Scarr, Dina   CM N
P.O. Box 500886
San Diego, CA 92150-0886
Tel: (619) 672-4317

Fingerhut, A. Tom   F
3470 Mt. Diablo Blvd Ste. A150
Lafayette, CA 94549
Tel: (510) 283-4692
Fax: (510) 283-1285

Folberg, Jay   F
2130 Fulton Street
San Francisco, CA 94117-1087
Tel: (415) 666-6307

Fritz, Roxanne CA, CM, F, S, N
1001 6th Street Ste. 203
Sacramento, CA 95814
Tel: (916) 446-0911
Fax: (916) 446-0932

Gomez, Patricia   CM, F
979 Osos Street Ste. 6-B
P.O. Box 15915
San Luis Obispo, CA 93406
Tel: (805) 544-8505
Fax: (805) 544-8505

Gross, Jeanice & Michael   F
4407 Manchester Ave. Ste 204
Encinitas, CA 92024
Tel: (619) 436-4100

Harrison, Frances L   F
1551 Fourth Avenue Ste. 700
San Diego, CA 92101
Tel: (619) 233-9500
Fax: (619) 237-8003

Healthier Divorce Services
Orli J. Peter   F
2445 Twentieth Street
Santa Monica, CA 90405
Tel: (310) 392-2534
Fax: (213) 965-7566

Henson, Laura   F
191 Calle Magdalena Ste. 280
Encinitas, CA 92024
Tel: (619) 685-9796

Holley, Vivian L.   F
1 Daniel Burnham Crt Ste 240
San Francisco, CA 94109
Tel: (913) 829-4927
Fax: (415) 441-8102

Huber, Karen E.   CM F N
567 San Nicolas, Ste. 304A
Newport Beach, CA 92660
Tel: (714) 640-2263

Hyde, Heather   F
501 Stockton Ave.
San Jose, CA 95126
Tel: (408) 995-6425
Fax: (408) 995-6427

Jackson, B./Coram, T.   CM F
5252 Balboa Avenue Ste. 604
San Diego, CA 92117
Tel: (619) 573-0173
Fax: (619) 573-0178

Jane Cassidy and Associates   F
6250 Merced Ave.
Oakland, CA 94611
Tel: (510) 339-7015
Fax: (510) 339-7020

Jones, Nancy Langdon   F
2485 Mesa Terrace
Upland, CA 91784
Tel: (909) 985-5550
Fax: (909) 985-9500
E-Mail: nancfp&cyberg8t.com

Jordan, Althea   F
385 Sherman Avenue #1
Palo Alto, CA 94306
Tel: (415) 325-8800
Fax: (415) 325-8837

Kelly & Associates
David Kelly/Andrea Kelly CM F
411 Oak Street
Roseville, CA 95678
Tel: (916) 782-8100
Fax: (916) 782-8121

Kresge, Jennifer   F
1308 Main Street, Ste. 114
St. Helena, CA 94574
Tel: (707) 963-5586

Lawrence, Lorraine/Wade, Jeff F
2718 5th. Ave
San Diego, CA 92103
Tel: (619) 299-0405
Fax: (619) 297-6221

Legal Alternatives
Laura Reindel   F
619 S. Vulcan Aveune #202
Encinitas, CA 92024
Tel: (619) 944-4120
Fax: (619) 942-5120

Lemmon Mediation Institute
John Lemmon   F
5248 Boyd Ave.
Oakland, CA 94618
Tel: (510) 547-8089

Lifeline Comm. Svc.   PF
Kim Mikhael   CM F S N
200 Jefferson Street
Vista, CA 92084
Tel: (619) 726-4900
Fax; (619) 726-6102

Litigation Alternatives
Evan Gould & Clive Essakow F
4350 Executive Drive Ste. 200
San Diego, CA 92121
Tel: (619) 824-9000
Fax: (619) 552-0261

Lund, Mary   F
2510 Main Street #201
Santa Monica, CA 90405
Tel: (310) 392-6163

Macfarlane, Robert F
1861 Parliament Road
Leucadia, CA 92024
Tel: (619) 753-3766

Mane Institute
Bruce Antman F
P.O. Box 241470
Los Angeles, CA 10026
Tel: (310) 474-2244

Mari Frank & Assoc. CM CA F
28202 Cabot Rd Ste 215
Lauguna Niguel, CA 92677
Tel: (714) 364-1511
Fax; (714) 363-7561

McCarter-Knight Mediation
Lanny Knight F S N
233 W. Shaw
Fresno, CA 93711
Tel: (209) 225-2510
Fax: (209) 225-2389

Mediation Center
Gail Nugent CM F S N
2183 Fairview Rd, Ste. 100
Costa Mesa, CA 92715
Tel: (714) 574-5990
Fax: (714) 574-5999

Mediation First
Barret Brown F
3576 Buttermilk Lane
Arcata, CA 95521
Tel: (707) 822-0490

Mediation Solutions
Steven Marlowe CA CM
31 North Second St. Ste. 300
San Jose, CA 95113
Tel: (888) 242-8844
Fax:(408) 371-5832

Mediation Association
Joel Edelman CM F S
169 Pier Avenue
Santa Monica, CA 90405
Tel: (310) 392-4830
Fax: (310) 392-6331

Mediation Ctr for Family Law
Nina R. Meierding F
857 E. Main Street
Ventura, CA 93001
Tel: (805) 643-3543
Fax: (805) 653-6107

Mellor, Dean J. F
1337 Ocean Ave.
Santa Monica, CA 90401
Tel: (310) 451-1004

Morgan, Louise Studrick F
519 Webster Street
San Francisco, CA 94117
Tel: (415) 552-8150
Fax: (415) 552-8150
E-Mail: lstrud@aol.com

Moss, Bleema F
3551 Front Street
San Diego, CA 92103
Tel: (619) 296-9401
Fax: (619) 291-0158

Mosten, F. /Tuffias,H. CM F
10990 Wilshire Blvd. #940
Los Angeles, CA 90024
Tel: (310) 473-7611
Fax: (310) 473-7422

Muenzer, Franklin B. CM
820 Manhattan Avenue Ste. 201
Manhattan Beach, CA 90266
Tel: (310) 372-0876
Fax: (310) 372-1240

Nixon, Judy F
1035 Minnesota Avenue Ste. G
San Jose, CA 95125
Tel: (408) 975-4690
Fax: (408) 975-4696

Olive Branch Counseling Center
K. Olson/S. DeJarnett CM F
9033 Baseline Road Ste. A
Rancho Cucamonga, CA 91730
Tel: (909) 989-9030
Fax: (909) 466-4594

Pacific Mediation Services
Janet Allen CM F S N
2223 Ave De La Playa Ste 212
La Jolla, CA 92037
Tel: (619) 459-4110
Fax: (619) 459-6434

Penn, Stephen W. F
16360 Monterey Road Ste. 120
Morgan Hill, CA 95037
Tel: (408) 776-1525
Fax: (408) 778-5447

Peterson, Sharon Shield   F
2067 First Aveune
San Diego, CA 92101
Tel: (619) 234-1388

Quinn-Hargreaves Med. Center
M. Quinn/Wm Hargreaves CM F
501 W. Broadway, Ste. 1720
San Diego, CA 92101
Tel: (619) 238-5501
Fax: (619) 235-4415

Resolution Remedies
Diane Levinson   CA CM F
14040 Civic Ctr Drive Ste. 200
San Rafael, CA 94903
Tel: (415) 492-2828
Fax: (415) 492-2872

Results Unlimited
Susan Creighton-Clavel   F
5777 Madison Ave. Ste. 120
Sacramento, CA 95841-3308
Tel: (916) 338-2230
Fax: (916) 487-9019

Rhoads, Donald Perry   CA CM
675 Grass Valley Road
Lake Arrowhead, CA 92352
Tel: (909) 336-2531
Fax: (909) 337-0329

Roberts, David   F
4283 Piedmont Avenue Ste. B
Oakland, CA 94611
Tel: (510) 655-1966

Roberts, Michael J. CA CM S N
401 West A Street Ste. 2350
San Diego, CA 92101
Tel: (619) 234-2588
Fax: (619) 234-1011

Robinson, Skip   CM
10800 Bodega Hwy.
Sebastopol, CA 95472-9501
Tel: (707) 824-8880
E-Mail: robinson@sonoma.edu

Rose, Chip   F
4340 Scotts Valley Dr. Ste. J
Scotts Valley, CA 95066-4541
Tel: (408) 438-1604
Fax: (408) 439-0703

Rouin, Carole   F
One World Trade Ctr Ste. 2320
Long Beach, CA 90831-2320
Tel: (310) 437-5409
Fax: (310) 437-4610

Russell, William R.   F
399 Sherman Avenue Ste. 3
Palo Alto, CA 94306
Tel: (415) 856-4800
Fax: (415) 473-4890

San Diego Presbytery Mediation
Tom Fentiman   CM F S N
8825 Arrow Drive Ste. 220
San Diego, CA 92123-2292
Tel: (619) 279-1001
Fax: (619) 279-0320

S. D. Volunteer Lawyer Prog.
Joan Thomas   F
225 Broadway #800
San Diego, CA 92101
Tel: (619) 235-5656 EXT: 109
Fax: (619) 235-5668

San Diego Mediation Center PF
625 Broadway Ste 1221 CM N F
San Diego, CA 92101
Tel: (619) 238-2400
Fax: (619) 238-8041

Schooler, Jane L.   CM F S N
1256 High Bluff Drive Ste. 290
San Diego, CA 92130
Tel: (619) 792-3533
Fax: (619) 755-8348

Schulman, D./Taylor, R.   F
2600 E. Nutwood, Ste. 250
Fullerton, CA 92831
Tel: (714) 871-8600
Fax: (714) 525-5405

Shomer, Evyn L.   F
517 Third Street Ste. 40
Eureka, CA 95501
Tel: (707) 442-8455
Fax: (707) 442-0756

Sierra Family Mediations
April Maynard/Mark Sussman F
149 Court Street
Auburn, CA 95603
Tel: (916) 888-6288
Fax: (916) 888-7364

Stivers, Nancy M.   F
2911 State Street Ste. I
Carlsbad, CA 92008
Tel: (619) 720-1874

The Bridge
J. Stanley Bunce   F
2926 North "G" Street Ste. 105
Merced, CA 95340
Tel: (209) 384-0414
Fax: (209) 384-1562

Todd, Marcia   F
6211 Telegraph Ave. #23
Oakland, CA 94609
Tel: (510) 420-8817
Fax: (510) 653-0729

Walker, Richard/Barbara   CM F
811 Coombs Street Ste. B
Napa, CA 94559
Tel: (707) 254-7515
Fax: (707) 254-7455

Webb, Jennifer   F
450 Newport Ctr. Dr. #250
Newport Beach, CA 92660
Tel: (714) 640-4095
Fax: (714) 721-8661

Weckstein, Donald   CA CM
S P.O. Box 9578
San Diego, CA 92169
Tel: (619) 483-0659
Fax: (619) 483-4669

Zelinsky, David   CM F
681 Main Street #104
Placerville, CA 95667
Tel: (916) 622-4351
Fax: (916) 622-5476

COLORADO
Acceptable Terms Med. Svc.
Roberta J. Steinhardt   F
5353 W. Dartmouth Ave Ste 401
Denver, CO 80227
Tel: (303) 988-5191

Arnold Swartz and Associates F
720 Kipling Street #200
Lakewood, CO 80215
Tel: (303) 237-4828
Fax: (303) 232-3892

CDR Associates   CM F S N
Bernard Mayer & Mary Golten
100 Arapahoe #12
Boulder, CO 80302
Tel: (303) 442-7367
Fax: (303) 442-7442

CDR Associates
Jean M. Bedell   F S
2142 Jordan Place
Boulder, CO 80304
Tel: (303) 443-4695
Fax: (303) 443-0599

Center for Solutions
Katherine S. Head   F
50 S. Steele St. Ste. 800
Denver, CO 80209
Tel: (303) 329-3435
Fax: (303) 299-5572

Coates, Christine A.   F
4890 Riverbend Rd
Boulder, CO 80301
Tel: (303) 443-8524
Fax: (303) 786-8035

Conflict Resolutions Inc.
Douglas S. Harrison   F
10600 W. Alameda #U-6
Lakewood, CO 80226
Tel: (303) 986-3100
Fax: (303) 986-3432

Dispute Management   CA CM
Daniel Himelspach   F S N
1660 Lincoln Ste. 2501
Denver, CO 80264
Tel: (303) 832-2090
Fax: (303) 832-2097

Eaton, Janet R.   F
102 South Tejon Street Ste. 750
Colorado Springs, CO 80903
Tel: (719) 636-5123
Fax: (719) 636-2077

Family Mediation Group
William Schwartz   F
709 Clarkson Street
Denver, CO 80218
Tel: (303) 322-3080
Fax: (303) 321-9473

Kerr, Linda Q.　　　　　　F
331 Lodgewood Lane
Lafayette, CO 80026
Tel: (303) 604-6321

McWilliams, Joan H.　　　　F
1775 Sherman St. Ste. 2825
Denver, CO 80203
Tel: (303) 830-0171
Fax: (303) 830-8422

Mediation West
Dixie N. Agnew　　　　　F
1000 Summit Blvd.
Frisco, CO 80443
Tel: (303) 668-3001
Fax: (303) 668-3108

Meltzer, Martin　　　　　F
6979 South Holly Circle Ste 190
Englewood, CO 80112
Tel: (303) 721-9779
Fax: (303) 721-7350

Meyrich, Steven　　　　　F
100 Arapahoe Ave. #14
Boulder, CO 80302
Tel: (303) 440-8238
Fax: (303) 938-9703

Nowak, Nancy Cohen　　　F
6966 S. Spruce Dr. West
Englewood, CO 80112
Tel: (303) 694-3132
Fax: (303) 337-4109

Paralegal Services & Mediation
Catherine M. Schultheis　　F
P.O. Box 103
Niwot, CO 80544
Tel: (303) 652-3638
Fax: (303) 652-3482

Rymers, John A.　　　　　F
1805 S. Bellaire St. Ste. 301
Denver, CO 80219
Tel: (303) 759-5103
Fax: (303) 757-4225

Taylor, Raymond　　　　　F
2004 N. 12th #4
Grand Junction, CO 81501
Tel: (303) 242-6061
Fax: (303) 243-8515

CONNECTICUT

Becker, Michael　　　　　F
2701 Summer St. Ste. 200
Stamford, CT 06905
Tel: (203) 263-2248
Fax: (203) 363-2249

Brakeman, Jill B.　　　　　F
62 Cook Street
Torrington, CT 06790
Tel: (860) 482-6900
Fax: (860) 489-3845

Center for Div. Med. & ADR
Mary or Walter Marcus　　F
10 Wall Street
Norwalk, CT 06852
Tel: (203)854-9394
Fax: (203) 454-0404
E-mail: ZWMZ@AOL.COM

Connecticut Ctr for Div. Med.
Martin Decker/John Miller　F
100 Market Square, Room 5
Newington, CT 06111
Tel: (860) 666-5110
Fax; (860) 665-8177

Ctr. for Div. Med. of Westrn CT.
Wendy Davenson/John Miller　F
88 Church Hill Road
Sandyhook, CT 06482
Tel: (203) 426-1997
Fax: (203) 426-1997

Davis, Jennifer　　　　　F
1098 Farmington Avenue
Bristol, CT 06010
Tel: (860) 589-4417
Fax: (860) 589-5780

Falco, Eugene P.　　　　　F
45 Church Street
New Hartford, CT 06057
Tel: (860) 379-7487
Fax: (860) 379-7487

Fried, Robert B.　　　　　F
2 Congress Street
Hartford, CT 06114-1024
Tel: (860) 728-6644
Fax: (860) 249-4073

Gravalec-Pannone, Kathleen　F
106 Williams Street
Norwich, CT 06360
Tel: (860) 885-1275

Hutton-Carney Mediation Assoc.
Carney, Mary Ann   F
360 Tolland Turnpike
Manchester, CT 06040
Tel: (203) 646-2535
Fax: (203) 643-1703

Institute of Living
Kenneth S. Robson   F
400 Washington St.
Hartford, CT 06106
Tel: (203) 241-6891
Fax: (203) 241-8045

Kennedy, George   CA CM F N
72 Slater Avenue
Jewett City, CT 06351
Tel: (860) 376-2567
Fax: (860) 376-0144

Levin, Juliana   CM F S N
200 Milford Point Road
Milford, CT 06460
Tel: (203) 877-2586

Linda L. Mariani & Associates F
83 Broad Street
New London, CT 06320-1630
Tel: (860) 443-5023
Fax: (860) 443-8897

Litigation Alternatives
Robert G. Yoles   CA CM
P.O. Box 270025
West Hartford, CT 06127-0025
Tel: (860) 521-8500
Fax: (860) 561-4533

Martin, Kathleen B.   F
79 Main Street
Unionville, CT 06085
Tel: (860) 673-7141
Fax: (860) 675-8955

Mediated Divorce Services
Carol Widing   F
185 Asylum Street Ste. 3100
Hartford, CT 06103
Tel: (203) 678-8401
Fax: (203) 678-8223

Mediation Center of Connecticut
Roberta S. Friedman   F
383 Orange St.
New Haven, CT 06511
Tel: (203) 776-9002
Fax: (203) 787-3259

Schaefer, Bernice C.   F
91 Duncaster Road
Bloomfield, CT 06002
Tel: (203) 243-9795
Fax: (203) 242-7097

Shapiro, Michael   CM F
39 Bristol Street
New London, CT 06320
Tel: (860) 444-1147
Fax: (860) 444-7456

Sienkiewicz, Nancy R.   F
9 South Main St.
New Millford, CT 06776
Tel: (203) 354-1583
Fax: (203) 355-4439

Strong, Leslie   F
46 Overlook Road
Glastonbury, CT 06033
Tel: (203) 633-6176
Fax: (203) 657-3531

Talbot, J/ Kirkwood, S   F
P.O. Box 1964
Torrington, CT 06790
Tel: (860) 489-9959
Fax: (860) 489-0916

Von Schmidt, Georgia   F
37 Arch Street
Greenwich, CT 06830
Tel: (203) 622-5900
Fax: (203) 622-8298

DIST. OF COLUMBIA
Business Mediation Associates
David Gage   CM
1301 20th Street, NW Ste. 603
Washington, DC 20036
Tel: (202) 363-1108
Fax: (202) 363-4087

Center for Mediation
Roger Lesser   F
1666 Conn. Ave NW Ste 250
Washington, D C 20009
Tel: (202) 797-7999
Fax: (202) 797-2354

Maida, Richard   F
6242 29th Street NW
Washington, D C 20015
Tel: (202) 362-2515
Fax: (202) 362-2515

Siler, Bernard   CM N
1207 Sheridan Street, NW
Washington, DC 20011
Tel: (202) 667-3664

DELAWARE
Affiliated Mediation Services
Sandra Taub/Phillip Facciolo   F
1813 Marsh Road
Wilmington, DE 19810
Tel: (302) 475-3114

Bookout, Anne   CA CM
P. O. Box 410
Wilmington, DE 19899-0410
Tel: (302) 652-8400
Fax: (302) 652-8405

Tressler Mediation Services
Jolly Clarkson-Shorter   F
1007 White Birch Drive
Newark, DE 19713
Tel: (302) 738-9702

FLORIDA
ADR Applications, Inc.
Nancy Yeend   CA CM F
100 Carillon Parkway Ste. 190
St. Petersburg, FL 33716
Tel: (800) 556-8808
Fax: (813) 556-0087
E-Mail: nyeend@ccb.com

Azan, Alex   F
11303 SW 24 Terrace
Miami, FL 33165-2254
Tel: (305) 348-2434
Fax: (305) 348-3950

Counseling and Mediation Ctr.
Larry B. Lake   F
P.O. Box 1379
St. Augustine, FL 32085
Tel: (904) 824-2501

DiGennaro, Iris B.   F
9131 College Pky Ste 13B
Fort Meyers, FL 33919
Tel: (813) 481-9683

Divorce & Family Mediation Ctr
Lee A. Schreiber   F
3949 Evans Ave. Ste. 206
Fort Meyers, FL 33901
Tel: (813) 936-5225
Fax: (813) 936-2542

Doelker, Richard E.   F
4555 Lavallet Lane
Pensacola, FL 32504
Tel: (904) 474-2688
Fax: (904) 474-3131

Dorian, Phyllis   F
3147 Hyde Park Drive
Clearwater, FL 34621
Tel: (813) 787-9627

Family Mediation Center
Donald R. Gillette   F
1006 North Armenia
Tampa, FL 33607
Tel: (813) 877-1210
Fax: (813) 876-5966

Gianino, Peter T.   F
217 East Ocean Blvd.
Stuart, FL 34994
Tel: (407) 286-0200
Fax: (407) 286-4789

Godard, Diane R.   F
3450 E. Lake Rd. Ste. 305
Palm Harbor, FL 34685
Tel: (813) 785-1820
Fax: (813) 781-5735

Kaslow Associates
Florence W. Kaslow   F
2161 Palm Beach Lakes Ste. 216
West Palm Beach, FL 33409
Tel: (407) 625-0288
Fax: (407) 832-3153

Koedam, Wilhelmina S.   F
1021 Ives Dairy Rd Bldg 3 #212
North Miami Beach, FL 33179
Tel: (305) 653-0098
Fax: (305) 654-4412

Percher, Martin L.   F
3752 Terrapin Land #2212
Coral Springs, FL 33067
Tel: (305) 344-0929

Rubin, Melvin A.   F
111 Majorca Avenue #A
Coral Gables, FL 33134
Tel: (305) 446-4630
Fax: (305) 446-4978

Sherr, Linda B.   F
504 Payne Parkway
Sarasota, FL 34237
Tel: (813) 955-1330
Fax: (813) 955-4163

Waxman, Geraldine Lee   F
9780 NW 16th Street
Plantation, FL 33322
Tel: (305) 472-7458
Fax: (305) 476-5677

GEORGIA
Atlanta Divorce Mediators
E. Elizabeth Manley   F
1149 Austin Ave. NE
Atlanta, GA 30307
Tel: (404) 378-3238
Fax: (404) 577-6505

Atlanta Divorce Mediators
Kathryn Marth   F
150 E. Ponce de Leon Ste. 460
Decatur, GA 30030
Tel: (404) 378-3238

Decision Management Assoc.
Robert A. Berlin   F
3081 Revere Court
Atlanta, GA 30340
Tel: (404) 455-7808
Fax: (404) 455-7272

Divorce Mediation of Cobb Cty.
Ted F. Simon   F
670 Village Trace, 19A #100
Marietta, GA 30067
Tel: (404) 980-0988
Fax: (404) 977-8899

Foster, Nancy   F
2321 Henry Clower Blvd. Ste. A
Snellville, GA 30278
Tel: (404) 979-0892
Fax: (404) 978-2255

Giese, Kay A.   F
P.O. Box 1626
Athens, GA 30603
Tel: (706) 549-0500
Fax: (706) 543-8453

Hair, Marcia E.   F
3350 Bryant Lane
Marietta, GA 30066
Tel: (404) 422-8815
Fax: (404) 977-2072

Keim, Timothy A.   F
7848 Princess Drive Court
Jonesboro, GA 30236
Tel: (770) 603-0506
Fax: (770) 473-0075

Kitchens, Marti P.   F
7193 Douglas Blvd. #103
Douglasville, GA 30135
Tel: (404) 942-9361
Fax: (404) 947-9840

Ma'luf, Jan   F
P.O. Box 3403
LaGrange, GA 30241-3403
Tel: (706) 883-2168
Fax: (706) 883-2169

Peaceful Resolutions Inc.
Norman M. Stoker   F
P.O. Box 813126
Smyrna, GA 30081-3126
Tel: (770) 432-0212

Schaffer, Beverly K.   F
1105-C Clairmont Ave.
Decatur, GA 30030
Tel: (404) 634-6394
Fax: (404) 727-4639

School for Dispute Resolution
Lemoine D. Pierce   F
P.O. Box 2372
Decatur, GA 30031-2372
Tel: (404) 299-1128
Fax: (404) 261-2017

HAWAII
Adam-Terem, Rosemary   F
1319 Punahou Street, #603
Honolulu, HI 96826
Tel: (808) 973-5418
Fax: (808) 973-8626
E-Mail: radamter@hawaii.edu

Bright, Valerie   F
73-1150 Oluolu Street
Kailua-Kona, HI 96740
Tel: (808) 322-2977

Chang, Louis   CM CA
900 Fort Street Ste. 310
Honolulu, HI 96822
Tel: (808) 524-4111
Fax: (808) 521-2389

Dispute Resolution Services
James Hoenig   CA CM F
1001 Bishop Street
Pauahi, HI 96813
Tel: (808) 523-1234
Tel: (808) 537-1377

Global Pacific Med. Svcs.
Sanford A. Mohr   CM F N S
P.O. Box 485
Kailua-Kona, HI 96745
Tel: (808) 325-0370
Fax: (808) 325-5608

Green, Tom   F
1188 Bishop Street #1306
Honolulu, HI 96813
Tel: (808) 526-1411
Fax: (808) 534-1015

IDAHO

Hawley, Victoria   F
3221 North 28th Street
Boise, ID 83703
Tel: (208) 336-9366
Fax: (208) 336-1451

Heartland Centers, Inc.
Patricia Crete Brown   F
303 N. 12th Ave.
Pocatelo, ID 83201
Tel: (208) 234-1099
Fax: (208) 234-1100

Knudson, Barbara   F
623 West Hays
Boise, ID 83702
Tel: (208) 336-1472

Thomas, Bruce   CA CM
802 W. Bannock Street Ste. 900
Boise, ID 83702
Tel: (208) 336-3250
Fax: (208) 336-9154

ILLINOIS

Bell, Herbert J.   F
5116 Forest Avenue
Downers Grove, IL 60515
Tel: (630) 971-2667
Fax: (630) 971-1488

Bell, Brigitte Schmidt CM F S N
53 W. Jackson Blvd. Ste. 702
Chicago, IL 60604
Tel: (312) 360-1124
Fax: (312) 360-1126

Berman, Myles   CA CM N
10 S. Wacker Drive Ste. 4000
Chicago, IL 60606-7407
Tel: (312) 715-4643
Fax: (312) 715-4800

Bongiorno & Associates
Margaret Rohde Bongiorno   F
417 West Roosevelt Road #10A
Wheaton, IL 60187
Tel: (630) 744-3450
Fax: (630) 871-3784

Borland, Kathleen Landreth   F
505 N. Lake Shore Dr. #2708
Chicago, IL 60611
Tel: (312) 345-8822
Fax: (312) 345-8801

Clipper, Robert C.   F
6464 West Main St. Ste. 6C
Belleville, IL 62223
Tel: (618) 397-9743

Common Sense Mediation
G. Schiesser/ V. Brubaker   F
1532 W. Victoria Street
Chicago, IL 60660-4223
Tel: (773) 506-1234
Fax: (773) 291-0911
E-Mail: gailschiesser@juno.com

DRB Alternatives, Inc.
Donna R. Bellafiore   F
608 S. Washington Street
Naperville, IL 60540
Tel: (630) 983-6801
Fax: (630) 983-6494

Dres, Demetri   F
6900 Main Street Ste. 120
Downer's Grove, IL 60516
Tel: (630) 969-0069
Fax: (630) 960-2941

Duffield, Brigid A.   F
1749 S. Naperville Rd Ste. 201
Wheaton, IL 60187
Tel: (630) 221-9300
Fax: (630) 221-9305

Family & Legal Social Services
Jacob, Lynn Carp   F
2234 Asbury Avenue
Evanston, IL 60201
Tel: (847) 866-6231
Fax: (847) 866-6718

Gay, Pat   F
P.O. Box 4322
Fairview Heights, IL 62208
Tel: (618) 277-1844

Gentry, Deborah Barnes   F
203 J Turner Hall
Normal, IL 61790-5060
Tel: (309) 438-7935
Fax: (309) 438-5037

Good, Diana G.   F
2123 O'Donnell Drive
Champaign, IL 61821
Tel: (217) 359-7052

Groselak, Bradley   F
15419 127th Street Ste. 100
Lemont, IL 60439
Tel: (630) 257-5816
Fax: (630) 257-8619

Habercoss & Associates
Karen Habercoss   F
1000 Jorie Blvd. Ste. 138
Oakbrook, IL 60521
Tel: (708) 656-1201

Hannah, Tamara   F
1861 North Bissell
Chicago, IL 60614
Tel: (312) 664-1338
Fax: (312) 664-1355

Harnish, Robert Brunk   F
736 Dobson St. #3E
Evanston, IL 60202
Tel: (708) 475-1642

Hogan, Judy L.   F
115 Campbell St. Ste. 100
Geneva, IL 60134
Tel: (708) 232-1886
Fax: (708) 232-1890

Kelly, Margaret   F
3841 West 95th Street
Evergreen Park, IL 60642
Tel: (708) 535-2777

Kennedy, Susan   F
2420 Isabella
Evanston, IL 60201
Tel: (708) 475-1059
Fax: (312) 527-0450

Kessler, Jerald A.   F
1950 Sheridan Rd. Ste. 101
Highland Park, IL 60035
Tel: (847) 433-2323
Fax: (847) 433-2349

London, William A.   F
4250 North Marine Dr. #402
Chicago, IL 60613
Tel: (312) 472-7673
Fax: (312) 975-0145

Massaquoi, Joan Elizabeth F
4940 E. End Ave. #2B
Chicago, IL 60615
Tel: (312) 947-9257
Fax: (312) 947-0381

McKee, M. Mark   F
43 Jefferson Ste 201
Naperville, IL 60540
Tel: (630) 357-8380
Fax: (630) 904-2251

Mediated Settlement Service
Lee Goodman   CA CM F
2201 Center Avenue
Northbrook, IL 60062
Tel: (847) 559-9525

Mediation Services of Mid-Il.
Bruce P. Mindrup   F
106 Goodrich Street
Jerseyville, IL 62052
Tel: (618) 498-4911
Fax: (618) 498-4921

Midwest Mediation Center
Erica Heyl   F
392 Lake Street
Antioch, IL 60002
Tel: (847) 395-1640
Fax: (847) 395-5891

PACTS
David Cavan Bruer   F
151 N. 4th St. #1
DeKalb, IL 60115
Tel: (815) 748-3237
Fax: (815) 748-5437

Partners In Transition
Nancee M. Blank   F
832 The Pines
Hinsdale, IL 60521
Tel: (708) 256-2300

Powers, Margaret S.   F
415 West Golf Rd. Ste. 22
Arlington Heights, IL 60005
Tel: (312) 943-2155 (x6)
Fax: (708) 670-0036

Sudduth, Debra   F
1906 Oakwood Ave.
Bloomington, IL 61704
Tel: (309) 664-0556
Fax: (309) 662-8821

The Marriage Doctors
Bob Hartley   CM F
520 N. Michigan, 7th Floor
Chicago, IL 60605
Tel: (312) 988-7900
E-Mail: belden502@aol.com

The Mediation Group
Frona C. Daskal   F
155 N. Michigan Ave. #700
Chicago, IL 60601
Tel: (312) 565-6565

INDIANA

Mitchell-Dix, Janet E.   F
5517 Oak Valley Place Ste. 205
Fort Wayne, IN 46845
Tel: (219) 483-7660
Fax: (219) 483-7660

Newton, Ann Kelly   F
501 North Arlington Street
Greencastle, IN 46135
Tel: (317) 653-3856
Fax: (317) 653-3856

Smith, Riette Thomas   F
P.O. Box 1965
Bloomington, IN 47402-1965
Tel: (812) 332-2558
Fax: (812) 332-2557

Strategies Inc.
Linda L. Long   F
460 Bote Drive
Porter, IN 46304
Tel: (219) 464-2940
Fax: (219) 926-4485

Tuttle, Deborah M.   F
300 N. Michigan Ste 219
South Bend, IN 46601
Tel: (219) 288-5100
Fax: (219) 282-4344

IOWA

Iowa Mediation Service
Mike Thompson   CA CM F S N
1025 Ashworth St. Ste. 202
West Des Moines, IA 50265
Tel: (515) 223-2318
Fax: (515) 223-2321

Iowa Peace Institute
Greg Buntz   CA CM F S N
917 10th Ave.
Grinnell, IA 50112
Tel: (515) 236-4880
Fax: (515) 236-6905
E-Mail: iapeacei@ac.grin.edu

Schultz, Louis   CA CM
1727 Brown Deer Road
Coralville, IA 52241
Tel: (319) 338-8095
Fax: (319) 338-8095

KANSAS

Counseling and Mediation Ctr.
Doug Morphis   F
334 North Topeka
Wichita, KS 67202
Tel: (316) 269-2322
Fax: (316) 269-2448

Fairchild, Robert W.   F
P.O. Box B
Lawrence, KS 66044
Tel: (913) 841-4700
Fax; (913) 843-0161

KENTUCKY

Colley, Rose T.   F
410 West Chestnut Ste. 356
Louisville, KY 40202-2323
Tel: (502) 581-1961
Fax: (502) 581-9832

Council on Peacemaking
Terry Weiss   F
1300 Willow Avenue
Louisville, KY 40204
Tel: (502) 581-1961
Fax: (502) 581-9832

Llewellyn, John   CA CM F S
3711 Hillsdale Road
Louisville, KY 40222
Tel: (502) 426-8161
Fax: (502) 581-1644

McCann, John D.   F
836 E. Euclid Avenue Ste. 317
Lexington, KY 40502
Tel: (606) 269-4525
Fax: (606) 268-9141

Mediation Professionals
Gayle & Herbert Warren   CM
125 S. 6th Street
Louisville, KY 40202
Tel: (502) 587-8136

Mediation First
Mark Stein   CM F
101 Crescent Avenue
Louisville, KY 40206
Tel: (502) 897-3020
Fax: (502) 899-1545
104224.32@compuserv.com

Parsons-Rulli, Peggy   F
2 Dortha Avenue
Florence, KY 41042
Tel: (606) 525-1487
Fax: (606) 525-7170

Zerhusen, Karen A.   F
178 Barnwood Drive Ste. 111
Edgewood, KY 41017
Tel: (606) 331-2558
Fax: (606) 344-1466

LOUISIANA
Family Mediation Center
Pamela G. Hansen   F
One Wood Street
Monroe, LA 71201
Tel: (318) 325-4881
Fax: (318) 324-0877

Mediation Center
Nell Lipscomb   F
3117 7th Street, Second Floor
Metairie, LA 70002
Tel: (504) 861-0505
Fax: (504) 838-7030

Mediation Center
Laura Prosser Davis   F
7737 Old Hammond Hwy # B-4
Baton Rouge, LA 70809
Tel: (504) 926-0776
Fax: (504) 926-0021

Morris, Edith H.   F
1515 Poydras St. Ste. 1870
New Orleans, LA 70112
Tel: (504) 524-3781
Fax: (504) 561-0228

Munger, Mary T.   F
4317 El Dorado
Metairie, LA 70006
Tel: (504) 887-5676

MAINE
Anthony, Cushman D.   F
P.O. Box 585
Portland, ME 04112
Tel: (207) 775-6371
Fax: (207) 871-1019

Mediation & Facilitation Res.
Jacqui Clark   F
71 Winthrop Street
Augusta, ME 04330
Tel: (207) 622-1429

MARYLAND
Crockett, Catherine Grayson F
401 E. Jefferson Street #108
Rockville, MD 20850
Tel: (301) 294-1380
Fax: (301) 294-7582

Curtis Associates Family Med.
Carolyn Curtis   F
408 Cranes Roost
Annapolis, MD 21401
Tel: (410) 757-7599
Fax: (410) 757-7599

Delphi Growth Solutions
Joel Hamaker   F N
P.O. Box 154
Glen Echo, MD 20812-0154
Tel: (301) 229-9470
Fax: (301) 229-9470

Family Center for Mediation
Sarah Childs Grebe   F
3514 Players Mill Road Ste. 100
Kensington, MD 20895
Tel: (301) 946-3400

183

Family & Child Associates
Phyllis B. Simon F
414 Hungerford Drive #240
Rockville, MD 20850
Tel: (301) 340-2060
Fax: (301) 984-3325

Girdner, Linda K. F
2324 Maytime Drive
Gambrills, MD 21054
Tel: (202) 662-1722
Fax: (202) 662-1755

Gorman, Nancy W. F
9042 Canterbury Riding
Laurel, MD 20723
Tel: (301) 498-1193
Fax: (301) 498-1193

Gorman, Powel Byrd F
318 Broadmoor Road
Baltimore, MD 21212
Tel: (410) 339-4655
Fax: (410) 296-7349

Hackett, Sylvia L. F
1701 Edmondson Ave. #202
Catonsville, MD 21228-4346
Tel: (410) 747-6840
Fax: (410) 788-1278

Halvorsen, Diane L. F
8018 Quarry Ridge Way
Bethesda, MD 20817
Tel: (301) 469-9637

Kraskin, Sara Dunham F
2 Wisconsin Court #700
Chevy Chase, MD 20815
Tel: (301) 654-4040
Fax: (301) 652-2148

Lifebridge Family Mediation
R. Ketcham & S. Sulami F
7104 Exfair Road
Bethesda, MD 20814
Tel: (301) 215-7933

Mediation Services of Annapolis
Martin Alan Kranitz F
1160 Spa Road 1-B
Annapolis, MD 21403
Tel: (800) 781-7500
Fax: (410) 974-8888

Mediation Resources
Martin Kobren F
7475 Wisconsin Ave. #500
Bethesda, MD 20814
Tel: (301) 718-2422

Murphy, Peter F. F
P.O. Box 119
Bryans Road, MD 20616
Tel: (301) 283-0947
Fax: (301) 375-8433

Potomac Mediation Group
Rachel S. Garron F
4919 Hampden Lane
Bethesda, MD 20814
Tel: (301) 652-6654

Quinlan, Robert E. F
8 Virginia Drive
Gaithersburg, MD 20877
Tel: (301) 840-2022
Fax: (301) 963-4105

Rodbell, Stanley L. F
10541 Catterskill Court
Columbia, MD 21044
Tel: (410) 730-2211
Fax: (410) 730-7618

Seymour, Shirley Pittman F
11907 Henry Fleet Drive
Potomac, MD 20854
Tel: (301) 340-1477
Fax: (301) 340-2942

Smith, David J. F
19 Kirwin Court
Parkville, MD 21234
Tel: (410) 836-4434
Fax: (410) 836-4198

Stovall, Lois H. F
P.O. Box 2123
Silver Spring, MD 20901
Tel: (301) 495-2991

Tong, Elizabeth B. F
108 North Washington Street
Easton, MD 21601
Tel: (410) 822-5993
Fax: (410) 822-5993

Vernon, Maureen F
3006 Solomons Island Road
Edgewater, MD 21037
Tel: (410) 266-0019
Fax: (410) 266-0019

Viertel, George CA CM
9525 Georgia Avenue Ste. 105
Silver Spring, MD 20910
Tel: (301) 589-7060
Fax: (301) 588-1763

Yee, Anna F
9219 Oregold Court
Laurel, MD 20708
Tel: (301) 725-3954
Fax; (301) 497-1966

MASSACHUSETTS

Balaschak, Elizabeth K. F
90 New State Highway
Raynham, MA 02767
Tel: (508) 823-4567
Fax: (508) 822-4097

Berkowitz, June F. F
73 Atlantic Road
Gloucester, MA 01930-3241
Tel: (508) 281-3910

Bowling, G. Daniel F
246 Long Pond Road
Great Barrington, MA 01230
Tel: (413) 528-5377

Dispute Mediation Inc.
Gail L. Perlman F
237 Main Street Ste. 4
Northampton, MA 01060-3139
Tel: (413) 585-0977
Fax: (413) 585-0999

Dispute Mediation Inc.
Bruce D. Clarkin F
95 State Street
Springfield, MA 01103
Tel: (413) 788-8981

Divorce Mediation Services
Diane Neumann F
650 Worcester Road
Framingham, MA 01701-5248
Tel: (508) 879-9095
Fax: (508) 879-9099

Fischer, S. Tracy F
99 Washington Street
Salem, MA 01970
Tel: (505) 745-0590
Fax: (508) 744-5151

Fish, Deborah Ann F
48 Doane Road
Chatham, MA 02633
Tel: (508) 945-3073
Fax: (508) 945-5022

Fiske, John F
189 Cambridge Street
Cambridge, MA 02141-1279
Tel: (617) 354-7133
Fax: (617) 354-5830

Franklin Mediation Service
Catherine Woolner F
97 Frankiin Street
Greenfield, MA 01301
Tel: (413) 774-7469
Fax: (413) 773-3834

Hantman, Elaine S. F
125 Water Street
Williamstown, MA 01267
Tel: (413) 458-4213

Kunstman, Earl F
68 South Main Street
Natick, MA 01760
Tel: (508) 651-2756
Fax: (508) 653-2271

New England Family Mediation
Carolyn Ross F
353 West Center St.
West Brigewater, MA 02379
Tel: (508) 559-0223
Fax: (508) 558-2067

The Mediation Group CM F S N
Brad & Jane Honoroff/D. Matz
3 Harvard Avenue, 2nd Floor
Brookline, MA 02146
Tel: (617) 277-9232
Fax: (617) 277-1699

Younger, Barbara C. F
161 Main Street
Wenham, MA 01984
Tel: (508) 468-2226
Fax: (508) 468-3801

MICHIGAN

Ann Arbor Center for the Family
Mary F. Whiteside   F
2300 Washtenaw Ave. Ste. 203
Ann Arbor, MI 48104
Tel: (313) 995-5181
Fax: (313) 995-9011

Ann Arbor Mediation Center
Gary Marsh & Zena Zumeta   F
330 E. Liberty #3A
Ann Arbor, MI 48104
Tel: (313) 663-1155
Fax: (313) 663-0524

Berecz , Debrorah L.   F
811 Ship St.
St. Joseph, MI 49085
Tel: (616) 983-0161
Fax: (616) 983-0166
E-Mail: berecz@andrews.edu

Dunigan, Linda L.   CM F
9400 S.W. Bay Shore Drive
Traverse City, MI 49684
Tel: (616) 929-3314

Kindt, Carol V.   F
207 W Grandview Pkwy Ste 102
Traverse City, MI 49684
Tel: (616) 935-1766

Mediation Works
Beverly Clark   F
440 E. Congress Ste 4R
Detroit, MI 48226-2917
Tel: (313) 961-4440
Fax: (313) 961-5830

Mikusko, M. Brady   F
330 E. Liberty Ste. 3A
Ann Arbor, MI 48104
Tel: (313) 663-1155

Nichols, Margaret J.   F
121 West Washington St. #300
Ann Arbor, MI 48104
Tel: (313) 994-3000
Fax: (313) 994-1557

Silver, Kenneth   CA CM
21599 W. 11 Mile Rd Ste 300
Southfield, MI 48076-3802
Tel: (810) 353-2882
Fax: (810) 353-4840

Williams, Carl E.   F
1860 Robert Street
Ann Arbor, MI 48104
Tel: (317) 846-4937

MINNESOTA

Ackerman, Mary   F
1725 Wellesley Avenue
St. Paul, MN 55105
Tel: (612) 690-3841
Fax: (612) 698-7222

Conflict Management Providers
Susan D. Mainzer   F
3033 Humboldt Avenue South
Minneapolis, MN 55408
Tel: (612) 824-7664
Fax: (612) 824-7664

Dispute Resolution Services
Christine M. Leick   F
120 S. 6th Street
Minneapolis, MN 55402
Tel: (612) 349-5252
Fax: (612) 349-9242

Elliason, Donald L.   F
3503 387th Street
Isle, MN 56342
Tel: (612) 676-3559

Erickson Mediation Institute
S. Erickson/ M. McKnight   F
850 Northland Plaza
3800 West 80th
Minneapolis, MN 55431
Tel: (612) 835-1564
Fax: (612) 835-3689

Family Conflict Resolution Ctr.
Dean A. Nyquist   F
5637 Brooklyn Blvd. #200
Brooklyn Center, MN 55429
Tel: (612) 533-7272
Fax: (612) 533-3183

Frederickson, Jeanette   F
3700 Piper Jaffray Tower
Minneapolis, MN 55402
Tel: (612) 339-7300
Fax: (612) 336-2940

Goodwyne, Lucille M.   F
5525 Timber Lane
Excelsior, MN 55331
Tel: (612) 470-0093

186

Hanson, Freya Ottem   F
625 Silver Lake Road
St. Paul, MN 55112
Tel: (612) 633-9408
Fax: (612) 633-1173

Hauksen, Terje   F
RR2, Box 17X
Pine Island, MN 55963
Tel: (507) 281-9295

Lakes Area Counseling & Med.
Marilyn J. Tisserand   F
110 6th Ave. East
Alexandria, MN 56308
Tel: (612) 763-9000

Mediation Center
Nancy Welsh   CA CM F
301 4th Ave. South Ste. 670
Minneapolis, MN 55415-1019
Tel: (612) 673-9555
Fax: (612) 341-7879
medctr.mhs.compuserve.com

Resolve
J. Kenneth Myers   CA CM S N
112 East Redwood Street
Marshall, MN 56258-1847
Tel: (507) 532-9222

MISSISSIPPI

Montjoy, R. Wilson   CA CM F
P.O. Box 119
Jackson, MS 39205
Tel: (601) 948-3101
Fax: (601) 960-6902
E-Mail: wmontjoy@brunini,com

Schwindaman, Dale   CA CM
P.O. Box 3439
Jackson, MS 39207-3439
Tel: (601) 353-3000
Fax: (601) 353-3007

MISSOURI

Alternative Solutions Inc.
Julius Z. Frager   F
13112 Piedmont Court
St. Louis, MO 63043
Tel: (314) 434-4200
Fax: (314) 434-2768

Amato, Susan L.   F
130 South Bemiston #302
Clayton, MO 63105
Tel: (314) 862-0330
Fax: (314) 727-5464

DeMarea & Associates Med.
Barbara A. DeMarea   F
10012 McGee Street
Kansas City, MO 64114-4141
Tel: (913) 384-1818

Families in Transition
Kakie Love   F
5413 Dalcross Drive
Columbia, MO 65203
Tel: (573) 443-7717
Fax: (573) 449-9505

Freed, Alan E.   F
165 N. Meramec, 6th Floor
Clayton, MO 63105
Tel: (314) 727-2266
Fax: (314) 727-2101

Kiser, Mary Anne   F
411 Nichols Road Ste. 217
Kansas City, MO 64112
Tel: (816) 931-9912
Fax: (816) 561-5352

Malley, Lynn M.   F
200 N. Ninth Street Ste. A
Columbia, MO 65201
Tel: (314) 499-0748
Fax: (314) 499-4469

Mediation Services of Missouri
ElGene Ver Dught   F
3600 S. Noland Rd Ste. A
Independence, MO 64055
Tel: (800) 637-7511
Fax: (816) 461-6022

Med. & Conflict Mangement
Robert D. Benjamin   CM F
8000 Bonhomme Ste. 201
St. Louis, MO 63105
Tel: (314) 721-4333
Fax: (314) 721-6845

Mulhearn, Michael   F
2100 N. Noland Road
Independence, MO 64050
Tel: (816) 254-9000
Fax: (816) 836-9922

Sher, Richard   CA CM S
10 S. Brentwood Blvd. Ste. 215
Clayton, MO 63105
Tel: (314) 721-1516
Fax: (314) 721-4434

Southwest Mediation Clinics
Michael L. Brockett   F
3937 College View Drive
Joplin, MO 64801
Tel: (417) 782-1846
Fax: (417) 782-4556

Stewart, Betsy Ann T.   F
1520-Q East 23rd St.
Independence, MO 64051
Tel: (816) 461-5858
Fax: (816) 461-2465

U. S. Arb. & Med. Midwest
Robert A. Crowe   CA CM
720 Olive Street Ste. 2020
St. Louis, MO 63101
Tel: (314) 231-4642
Fax: (314) 231-2357

MONTANA
Andes, Roy H.   F
305 E. Alder Street
Missoula, MT 59802
Tel: (406) 728-7295

Montana Mediators
Arthur Lusse/Katherine Lusse   F
201 West Main St. Ste. 104
Missoula, MT 59802
Tel: (406) 543-1113
Fax: (406) 543-1157

NEBRASKA
Lamberty, Patricia A.   CM F
320 North 68th Street
Omaha, NE 68132
Tel: (402) 556-5808
Fax: (402) 558-1929

NEVADA
A Peaceful Solution
Morrisa Schechtman   F
2810 W. Charleston Blvd # G69
Las Vegas, NV 89102
Tel: (702) 870-3000
Fax: (702) 384-5250

Alternative Solutions
Charlotte S. Kiffer   F
333 North Rancho Drive #138
Las Vegas, NV 89106
Tel: (702) 646-2645

Ashleman, Ivan   CA CM
550 E. Charleston
Las Vegas, NV 89104
Tel: (702) 387-6156
Fax: (702) 387-8823

Bengtson, Patti   F
2359 Wide Horizon Drive
Reno, NV 89509
Tel: (702) 328-3830

Clark Co. Nghbrhd Justice Ctr.
Ruth Pearson Urban   F PF
1600 Pinto Lane
Las Vegas, NV 89106
Tel: (702) 455-5722
Fax: (702) 455-5950

Coyne, Patricia Hellmund   F
300 South 4th Street #611
Las Vegas, NV 89101
Tel: (702) 384-1700
Fax: (702) 384-8150

Family Mediation Program
Phil Bushard   F
75 Court Street
Reno, NV 89501
Tel: (702) 328-3556
Fax: (702) 328-3548

Georges, Jean   CM
701 Rancho Circle
Las Vegas, NV 89107-4619
Tel: (702) 870-0805
Fax: (702) 870-0118

Howard, Dorothy A.   F
408 Ackerman Lane
Henderson, NV 89014
Tel: (702) 731-8134
Fax: (702) 731-5209

Meyer, Joy D.   F
6200 South Virginia Street
Reno, NV 89511
Tel: (702) 851-0913
Fax: (702) 828-6200

188

Rivard, Charlene   F
5317 Westleigh
Las Vegas, NV 89102
Tel: (702) 878-5396

NEW HAMPSHIRE
Atlternative Center for Med.
Olivia A. Ruel   F
4 Felt Road
Keene, NH 03431
Tel: (800) 891-7931
Fax: (603) 358-1081

Divorce & Family Mediation
Francoise Elise   F
114 Bay Street
Manchester, NH 03104
Tel: (603) 627-0525
Fax: (603) 627-0525

Nashua Mediation Program
Candace Dochstader   F
18 Mulberry Street
Nashua, NH 03060
Tel: (603) 594-3330
Fax: (603) 594-3452

New Hampshire Mediation
Rose M. Hill   F
280 Pleasant Street, H-3
Concord, NH 03301-2553
Tel: (603) 224-8043
Fax: (603) 224-8388

NEW JERSEY
Adv Approach Ctr for Div Med
Robert A. Lee   F
642 Van Emburgh Avenue
Wash. Township, NJ 07675
Tel: (201) 666-2550
Fax: (201) 722-8935

Agreement Zone
Tom Fee   C A F S N
100 Route 33 West
Freehold, NJ 07728-2543
Tel: (908) 866-1932
Fax: (908) 866-1942
E-Mail: tomfee@aol.com

Alternative Divorce Med. Ctr.
Michael Bateman   F
2130 Highway 35 Ste. 121-A
Sea Girt, NJ 08750
Tel: (908) 974-8889
Fax: (908) 974-1463

Bean, Ralph   F
145 Wellington Avenue
Pleasantville, NJ 08232
Tel: (609) 484-9736
Fax: (609) 748-5515

Forlenza, Samuel G.   F
207 Manor Aveune
Harrison, NJ 07029-2017
Tel: (201) 621-5060

Hillman, Gail   F
100 Northfield Avenue
West Orange, NJ 07052
Tel: (201) 669-2811
Fax: (201) 669-2838

Holman, Adele M.   F
95 Dana Place
Englewood, NJ 07631-3629
Tel: (201) 567-2202

Kressel, Kenneth   F
324 Raritan Avenue
Highland Park, NJ 08904
Tel: (908) 572-5444

Margulies, Sam   F
45 Park Street
Montclair, NJ 07042
Tel: (201) 783-5515
Fax: (201) 655-0016

Muise, Madeline   F
104-110 Maple Avenue
Red Bank, NJ 07701
Tel: (908) 530-2951
Fax: (908) 576-8197

Mediation Associates
Robert J. Farley   F
31 Greenbrook Drive
West Milford, NJ 07480
Tel: (201) 728-5427

Simpson, Gerald   F
229 Washington Street
Toms River, NJ 08753
Tel: (908) 244-5300
Fax: (908) 244-6745

Wells, Mary Vivian   F
36 June Place
Matawan, NJ 07747
Tel: (908) 583-1620
Fax: (908) 583-5532

NEW MEXICO

Anothy, Kathleen Burke   F
P.O. Box 26721
Albuquerque, NM 87125-6721
Tel: (505) 256-2552

Beyer, Roberta   F
1228 Central SW
Albuquerque, NM 87102
Tel: (505) 243-1761
Fax: (505) 243-3567

Drew, Walter   CA CM S N
3918 Old Santa Fe Trail
Santa Fe, NM 87505
Tel: (505) 982-9797
Fax: (505) 982-9797

Johnston, Retta   F
Route 4, Box 15C
Santa Fe, NM 87501
Tel: (505) 982-2983

N. M. Ctr for Dispute Resolution
Jean Ann Sidwell   F
1520 B Paseo de Peralta
Santa Fe, NM 87501
Tel: (505) 988-4578

Welsh, Mary McAnaw   F
P.O. Box 3483
Las Cruces, NM 88003
Tel: (505) 522-3066

NEW YORK

Abel, Steven L.   F
2 New Hempstead Road
New City, NY 10956
Tel: (914) 633-4283
Fax: (914) 634-1675

Albany Family & Divorce
Mediation Lisa Gordon   F
16 Groesbeck Place
Delmar, NY 12054
Tel: (518) 439-6900
Fax: (518) 439-8233

Angelini, Constance J.   F
3809 Snowden Hill Road
New Hartford, NY 13413
Tel: (315) 737-9287

Barsky, Morna   F
877 Lorenz Avenue
Baldwin, NY 11510
Tel: (516) 223-2025

Buffalo Mediation Associates
Charlene K. Brumley   F
4367 Harlem Road
Amherst, NY 14226
Tel: (716) 839-0040
Fax: (716) 839-1983

Community Mediation Services
Mark Kleiman   F
89-64 163rd Street
Jamaica, NY 11432
Tel: (718) 523-6868 EXT 248
Fax: (718) 523-8204

Ctr. for Family & Divorce Med.
Howard Yahm   F
146 Willow Tree Road
Monsey, NY 10952
Tel: (914) 354-3158
Fax: (212) 721-1012

Ctr. for Family & Divorce Med.
Kenneth Neumann   F
111 West 90th St. Townhouse B
New York, NY 10024
Tel: (212) 799-4302
Fax: (212) 721-1012

Dispute Mediation Program
Robert C. Niles   CM F S N
51 Kenaware Ave.
Delmar, NY 12054
Tel: (518) 439-3404
Fax: (518) 271-1909
SNKS82A@prodiqy.com

Divorce and Family Resource
Mary N. Miller   F
43-31 223rd Street
Bayside, NY 11361
Tel: (718) 631-0156
Fax: (718) 631-0154

Divorce Mediation Associates
Dolly Hinckley   F
47 Round Trail Drive
Pittsford, NY 14534
Tel: (716) 381-4841
Fax: (716) 381-4841

Div. Med. Ctr. of Suffolk Cty.
Lawrence C. Gulino   F
Four Freshman Lane
Stony Brook, NY 11790
Tel: (516) 751-3813

Divorce Med. Ctr of Long Island
Emanuel Plesent   F
340 A Willis Avenue
Mineola, NY 11501
Tel: (516) 747-1344
Fax: (516) 747-4489

Family Mediation Center
Roger S. Reid   F
7000 East Genesee St., Bldg. B
Fayetteville, NY 13066
Tel: (315) 446-5513
Fax: (315) 446-5513

Family & Divorce Mediation
Susan J. Brown   F
319 North Tioga Street
Ithaca, NY 14850
Tel: (607) 272-8837

Fay, Deborah   F
P.O. Box 938
Mahopac, NY 10541
Tel: (914) 628-9224
Fax: (914) 628-8009
E-Mail: debbie@cloud9.net

Friedman, Doris Toltz   F
11 Martine Avenue
White Plains, NY 10606
Tel: (914) 997-6363
Fax: (914) 997-2143

Gardner, Nancy   F
10 Riverview Place
Hastings-On-Hudson, NY 10706
Tel: (914) 478-2973
Fax: (914) 478-1493

Gateway Mediation Service
Naomi S. Eckhaus   F
56 Hutchinson Blvd.
Scarsdale, NY 10583
Tel: (914) 725-1244

Goodwin, Walter W.   F
12 Princess Lane
Londonville, NY 12211
Tel: (518) 434-1891

Hamma, Judith M.   F
54 Brookline Avenue
Elmira, NY 14905
Tel: (607) 733-2765

Handin, Kenneth H.   F
18 Seeley Drive
Albany, NY 12203
Tel: (518) 573-3561

Hickey, M. Christine   F
719 East Genesee St. Ste. 225
Syracuse, NY 13210
Tel: (315) 422-9756

Keiser, Susan   F
149 Main St.
Livingston Manor, NY 12758
Tel: (914) 439-5550
Fax: (914) 439-5554

Kimmelman, Donald M.   F
14 Balmville Lane
Newburgh, NY 12550-1422
Tel: (914) 561-1087

Levine, Barbara S.   F
2701 Rosendale Road
Schenedtady, NY 12309
Tel: (518) 377-2802

Lewin, Vicki   F
11 North Goodman Street
Rochester, NY 14607
Tel: (716) 244-1600
Fax: (716) 473-6683

Marshall, Lorraine   F
200 Mamaroneck Avenue
White Plains, NY 10601
Tel: (914) 428-1040
Fax: (914) 428-1595

Matrimonial Mediation Center
Ross T. Runfola   F
420 Franklin Street
Buffalo, NY 14202
Tel: (800) 888-5288
Fax: (716) 885-3369

Mediation Alternative
Daine Yale   F
4465 Douglas Avenue #10G
Riverdale, NY 10471-3523
Tel: (718) 601-6265
Fax: (718) 601-6455

191

Mediation Services
Helvi McClelland   F
16 North Goodman Street #113
Rochester, NY 14607
Tel: (716) 473-8723
Fax: (716) 473-7711

Mediation Network of Syracuse
Ronald W. Heilmann   F
1940 Valley Drive
Syracuse, NY 13207
Tel: (315) 492-1082

Mediation Services Inc.
Barbara J. Potter   F
48 Dietz Street Ste. 1
Oneonta, NY 13820
Tel: (607) 433-1672

Mediation Center
Patricia A. Connelly   F
1741 Route 9
Clifton Park, NY 12065
Tel: (518) 371-6830

Mediation Services
Lorraine H. Pantaleo   F
21 Hilltop Drive
Chappaqua, NY 10514
Tel: (914) 238-5150

Mediation Center of Rochester
John Heister & Anne Blaise   F
2024 West Henrietta Road #5G
Rochester, NY 14623
Tel: (716) 272-1990
Fax: (726) 272-1978

Mid-Hudson Div. and Family
Med. Jill Lundquist   F
P.O. Box 23
Barrytown, NY 12507
Tel: (914) 471-7167
E-Mail: lbaz@aol.com

Mid-Hudson Div. & Family
Med. Kathryn S. Lazar   F
110 Route 82
Hopewell Junction, NY 12533
Tel: (914) 896-9651

Miller, Marilyn A.   F
1221 East Genesee Street
Syracuse, NY 13210
Tel: (315) 428-1221

Milowe, Joan   F
3 Construction Drive
Glenmont, NY 12077
Tel: (518) 439-1314

New York Mediation Group
Sally Ganong Pope   F
23 West 73rd Street
New York, NY 10023
Tel: (212) 721-0770
Fax: (212) 721-0773

Norton, Nancy   F
26 Quarry Road
Ithaca, NY 14850
Tel: (607) 272-0556

Sanders-Demott, Jill   F
91 Hillside Drive
Mahopac, NY 10541
Tel: (914) 621-1231

Scher, Steve   F
82 Hart Blvd.
Staten Island, NY 10301
Tel: (718) 727-2901

Shanok, Susan Whiting   F
324 W. 22nd St. #PH
New York, NY 10011
Tel: (212) 242-4194
Fax: (212) 645-0392

Shapiro, Deanna S.   F
RD #1, Box 728
Croton-On-Hudson, NY 10520
Tel: (914) 271-4947

Shequine, Elizabeth K.   F
17 Collegeview Avenue
Poughkeepsie, NY 12603
Tel: (914) 471-2039
Fax: (914) 486-4080

Sloan, Sydell   F
17-26 215 Street
Bayside, NY 11360
Tel: (718) 631-1600
Fax: (718) 423-0325

Stallman, Peggy   F
21 Carol Drive
Mt. Kisco, NY 10549
Tel: (914) 666-6708
Fax: (914) 666-6708

192

Stillman, Philip   F
2781 Rosedale Road
Schenectady, NY 12309
Tel: (518) 370-4645

Weiner, Judith   F
10 Patricia Lane
White Plains, NY 10605
Tel: (914) 997-1222

NORTH CAROLINA

Albert, Lynne   CA CM
3100 Tower Blvd Ste. 1200
Durham, NC 27707
Tel: (919) 490-0500
Fax: (919) 490-0873

Baroff, Roy   CM
P.O. Box 847
Raleigh, NC 27602
Tel: (919) 833-1283
Fax: (919) 833-1059

Cochran, Sherry M.   F
3216 Bedford Avenue
Raleigh, NC 27607
Tel: (919) 828-4001

Cox, M. Susan   F
6821 Dumbarton Drive
Charlotte, NC 28210
Tel: (708) 556-9030

Family Counseling & Med.   F
108 W. Kime Street
Burlington, NC 27215
Tel: (919) 227-8412

Kahn, Annette L.   F
25 B Mount Bolus Road
Chapel Hill, NC 27514
Tel: (919) 967-1291
Fax: (919) 967-3336

Livermore, Jean Randle   F
18 W. Colony Place #250
Durham, NC 27705
Tel: (919) 493-2674 EXT 106
Fax: (919) 493-1923

Mediation Inc. of North Carolina
Larry Kimel   CA CM F
14 Clayton Street
Asheville, NC 28801
Tel: (704) 253-9300
Fax: (704) 251-0303

Mediation Center
Paul R. Smith   F
189 College Street
Asheville, NC 28801
Tel: (704) 251-6089
Fax: (704) 251-6061

Neville, William G.   F
10 Cogswood Road
Asheville, NC 28804
Tel: (704) 254-1058
Fax; (704) 252-2180

O'Briant, Celia   F
2711 D Pinedale Road
Greensboro, NC 27408
Tel: (919) 282-0052

Price, George L.   F
603 Surry Road
Chapel Hill, NC 27514
Tel: (919) 942-6937
Fax: (919) 942-6937

Resolve! Associates
Scott Bradley   F
P.O. Box 282
Chapel Hill, NC 27514-0282
Tel: (919) 929-6333
Fax: (919) 967-1886

OHIO

AAL Mediation
Lou Ann Reed   F
6726 Main Street
Newtown, OH 45244
Tel: (513) 271-4187

Beech Acres Aring Institute
Marie Hill & Donna Dansker
Sally Brush   F
6881 Beechmont Avenue
Cincinnati, OH 45230
Tel: (513) 231-7205 EXT 295
Fax: (513) 624-0134

Blalock, Susan T.   F
2535 Brandon Road
Columbus, OH 43221
Tel: (614) 486-7200

Ctr. for Resolution of Disputes
Jerry Lawson   CA CM F
8 W. Ninth Street
Cincinnati, OH 45202
Tel: (513) 721-4466
Fax: (513) 721-3383

193

Creative Resolutions
Judith Wayne Thomas   F
4 Sheppard Place
Granville, OH 43023
Tel: (614) 587-3367
Fax: (614) 587-2798

Crittenton Family Services
Janice Beaty & Jim Rundle   F
1414 E. Broad Street
Columbus, OH 43205
Tel: (614) 251-0103
Fax: (614) 251-1177

Eisenstein, Bette D.   F
24400 Highpoint Road
Beachwood, OH 44122
Tel: (216) 360-0776
Fax: (216) 360-0358

Frank, Sandra Hosmer   F
2137 Scottwood
Toledo, OH 43620
Tel: (410)·422-3711

Jewish Family Service Assoc.
Jane Hill/Phyllis Hulewat   F
24075 Commerce Park
Beachwood, OH 44122
Tel: (216) 292-3999
Fax: (216) 292-6313

Johnson, Sandra   F
5480 F Winding Way
Columbus, OH 43220
Tel: (216) 329-5290

Kline, Annette E.   F
107 E. Spruce Avenue
Ravenna, OH 44266
Tel: (216) 296-1949

Kolman, Marya Cody   F
731 E. Broad Street
Columbus, OH 43205
Tel: (614) 221-1058
Fax: (614) 228-1135

Lang, Michael D.   F
800 Livermore Street
Yellow Springs, OH 45387
Tel: (513) 767-6321
Fax: (513) 767-6461

Lansky, Dona T.   F
3758 Clifton Avenue
Cincinnati, OH 45220
Tel: (513) 751-0392
Fax: (513) 751-0392

Larsen, Bea V.   F
30 Garfield Place #920
Cincinnati, OH 45202
Tel: (513) 241-9844
Fax: (513) 241-9908

LeVine, Shoshana D.   F
2522 Highland Avenue
Cincinnati, OH 45219
Tel: (513) 221-8545
Fax: (513) 861-2724

Maumee Valley Mediation
Denise Herman McColley   F
105 West Main Street
Napoleon, OH 43545
Tel: (419) 599-5880
Fax: (419) 599-2873

Motz, Frank J.   F
4450 Belden Vlg. St NW # 213
Canton, OH 44718
Tel: (216) 492-4004

Ohio Dispute Resolution
Stanley Hanover   CM
7031 Wilson Mills Road
Chesterland, OH 44026 ·
Tel: (216) 423-1959
Fax: (216) 423-1959

Partners in Mediation
Margaret Reis & Barbara Doll F
30 E. Central Parkway Ste. 1200
Cincinnati, OH 45202
Tel: (513) 651-1010
Fax: (513) 421-3455

Petersen, Virginia   F
595 Copeland Mill Road
Westerville, OH 43082
Tel: (614) 794-2145
Fax: (614) 794-0579

Plowshares
Martha Green   F
12890 TWP Road 64
Glenford, OH 43739
Tel: (614) 659-2322
Fax: (614) 659-2322

194

Quinn, John & Maggie   F
1006 Hatch Street
Cincinnati, OH 45202
Tel: (513) 579-1006

Rauh, Trudy D.   F
617 Vine Ste., 1409
Cincinnati, OH 45202-2422
Tel: (513) 621-9100
Fax: (513) 345-5543

Readey, James   CA CM
21 West Broad Street, 9th Floor
Columbus, OH 43215
Tel: (614) 221-3377

Slovin, Sherri Goren   F
30 Garfield Place #920
Cincinnati, OH 45202
Tel: (513) 241-9844
Fax: (513) 241-9908

Solomon, Victoria E.   F
462 Gresham Drive
Fairlawn, OH 44333
Tel: (216) 665-1496

Swenson, Elizabeth   F
20700 North Park Blvd
University Heights, OH 44118
Tel: (216) 397-4434
Fax: (216) 397-1633

Swift, Leslie H.   F
1 Triangle Park Drive #101
Sharonville, OH 45246
Tel: (513) 672-3500
Fax: (513) 672-3503

Wallace, Evelyn Marie   F
4039 Rose Hill Avenue
Cincinnati, OH 45229
Tel: (513) 281-8419
Fax: (513) 281-0501

OKLAHOMA
Conner, Leslie, Jr.   CA CM
6801 N. Broadway Ext. #205
Oklahoma City, OK 73116-9037
Tel: (405) 843-1404
Fax: (405) 843-1495

Dispute Resolution Consultants
Joseph Paulk   CA CM
2021 S. Lewis #250
Tulsa, OK 74104
Tel: (918) 743-7151
Fax: (918) 749-8306

Hulett, Carrie S.   F
119 N. Robinson #1100
Oklahoma City, OK 73102
Tel: (405) 232-3407
Fax: (405) 232-3461

Riley, Ann T.   F
110 N. Mercedes Ste. 400
Norman, OK 73069
Tel: (405) 366-6100
Fax: (405) 329-1615

Rineer, Hugh   F
2900 Boatmens Center
Tulsa, OK 74119
Tel: (918) 583-1818
Fax: (918) 587-8537

OREGON
Atkin, Joe   F
1050-G Crater Lake Avenue
Medford, OR 97504
Tel: (503) 776-9166

Bridges, Lynda   F
2040 Commerical Street SE
Salem, OR 97302
Tel: (503) 364-2016
Fax: (503) 364-2585

Bryen, Gloria S.   F
14060 SW Maverick Court
Beaverton, OR 97008
Tel: (503) 644-1027

Cohen, Stanley N.   F
1119 NW 1st Street
Dundee, OR 97115
Tel: (503) 538-7982
Fax: (503) 538-7982

Coleman, Ben   F
1698 Liberty Street SE
Salem, OR 97302
Tel: (503) 363-5487
Fax: (503) 363-5487

Common Ground Mediation
Kathleen A. Mounts   F
1033 Forrester Way
Eugene, OR 97401
Tel: (503) 342-2388

Davis, Robert   CA CM N
1830 NE D Street
Grants Pass, OR 97526
Tel: (541) 479-2338
Fax: (541) 479-2087
E-Mail: dkdusac@magic.net

Family Mediation Center
Lois Gold   F
1020 SW Taylor #650
Portland, OR 97205
Tel: (503) 248-9740
Fax: (503) 295-0814

Gartland, John C.   F
P.O. Box 11230
Eugene, OR 97440-3430
Tel: (503) 344-2174
Fax: (503) 344-0209

Hal Harding Mediation Svc. F
312 SW Jefferson
Corvallis, OR 97339
Tel: (503) 757-7594
Fax: (503) 757-1310

Kadish, Joshua D.   F
900 SW 5th Avenue #1900
Portland, OR 97204
Tel: (503) 228-8448
Fax: (503) 273-9135

Mediation Center   F
Jim Melamed/Kathleen Corcoran
440 E. Broadway Ste. 340
Eugene, OR 97401
Tel: (541) 345-1456
Fax: (541-345-4024

Mediation Services
Pat Dixon   F
2695 12th Place SE
Salem, OR 97302
Tel: (503) 363-8075
Fax: (503) 391-5348

Nolan, Barbara C.   F
19157 Willamette Drive
West Linn, OR 97068
Tel: (503) 635-2123

Reiman, John W.   F
P.O. Box 474
Monmouth, OR 97361
Tel: (503) 753-4667
Fax: (503) 838-8150

Salem Med. and Counseling
W. Suzanne Warren   F
1764 37th Avenue NW
Salem, OR 97304
Tel: (503) 363-0316
Fax: (503) 363-0316

Scher, Linda R.   F
1500 SW First Avenue #630
Portland, OR 97201
Tel: (503) 226-7986
Fax: (503) 223-0743

Silverman, Peter   F
111 Bush Street
Ashland, OR 97520
Tel: (503) 776-7171 EXT 198

Slezak, Ingrid   F
1000 SW Broadway Ste. 1710
Portland, OR 97205
Tel: (503) 223-2671
Fax: (503) 223-0402

Spier, Richard   CA CM
2121 NE 17th Avenue
Portland, OR 97212-4602
Tel: (503) 284-2511
Fax: (503) 284-2519

Taylor, Alison Y.   F
P.O. Box 1131
Hillsboro, OR 97123
Tel: (503) 640-0731
Fax: (503) 640-0731

Teamwork for Children
Jeanne Etter   F
85444 Teague Loop
Eugene, OR 97405
Tel: (503) 342-2692
Fax: (503) 342-2692

Thurlow, Diane   F
217 Grest Drive
Eugene, OR 97405
Tel: (503) 342-2388

PENNSYLVANIA

Blumstein, Ed   CA CM F
1518 Walnut 4th Floor
Philadelphia, PA 19151
Tel: (215) 790-9666
Fax: (215) 790-1988

Bollenbacher, Lisa   F
71 Cypress Place
Newtown, PA 18940
Tel: (215) 504-9538
Fax: (215) 504-5329

C. A. Hughes and Associates
Carol A. Hughes   F
410 Maple Ave.
Greensburg, PA 15601
Tel: (412) 836-1214
Fax: (412) 836-6197
E-Mail: carolpsych@aol.com

Central Penn. Mediation
Services Arnold T. Shienvold   F
2151 Linglestown Road Ste. 200
Harrisburg, PA 17110
Tel: (717) 540-9005
Fax: (717) 540-1416

Cohen, Nancy S.   F
1760 Market St. Ste. 700
Philadelphia, PA 19103
Tel: (215) 575-9140
Fax: (215) 386-1743

Connors, Robin   F
310 Grant Street
Pittsburgh, PA 15219
Tel: (412) 391-4000
Fax: (412) 391-8518

Edward Blumstein & Assoc.   F
1518 Walnut Stret ,4th Floor
Philadelphia, PA 19102
Tel: (215) 790-9666
Fax: (215) 790-1988

Ferrell and Associates, Inc.
D. K. Ferrell   F
111 North Franklin Street
Wilkes-Barre, PA 18701
Tel: (717) 826-0999
Fax: (717) 825-1227
E-Mail: fl02150@epix.net

Hanna, Edward   F
661 Reading Avenue
West Reading, PA 119611
Tel: (610) 373-5005

Judicate   CA CM
200 S. Broad St Ste. 800
Philadelphia, PA 19102
Tel: (215) 546-6200
Fax: (215) 546-8567

Klitsch, Eileen Schanel   F
252 South State Street
Newtown, PA 18940
Tel: (215) 860-5533
Fax: (215) 276-6292

Langton, Dorothy   F
601 Walnut Street
Phildelphia, PA 19106
Tel: (215) 592-9060
Fax: (215) 928-0659

Latman, Carrie C.   F
2130 Penn Avenue
West Lawn, PA 19609
Tel: (610) 678-4410

Lehigh Valley Mediation Inc.
Don Stephen Klein   F
1436 Hampton Road
Allentown, PA 18104
Tel: (610) 395-7933

Marcus, Patricia R.   F
145 E. Market Street
York, PA 17401
Tel: (717) 852-7272
Fax: (717) 852-7360

McGalliard, David W.   CM F
638 Newtown-Yardley Rd # 1-G
Newtown, PA 18940
Tel: (215) 860-9742

Mediation Masters
Paul Wahrhaftig   F
7514 Kensington Street
Pittsburgh, PA 15221
Tel: (412) 371-1000
Fax: (412) 481-5601

Mediation Masters
E. Sherle Josephs   F
134 W. Lyndhurst Drive
Pittsburgh, PA 15206
Tel: (412) 371-1000
Fax: (412) 481-5601

Mediation Services
Patricia B. Wisch   F
1601 Walnut Street Ste. 1424
Philadelphia, PA 19102
Tel: (215) 988-9104

Morton, Kim Denise   F
220 West Gay Street
West Chester, PA 19380
Tel: (610) 431-4500
Fax: (610) 430-8718

Neely, Victoria Petro   F
1546 McDaniel Drive
West Chester, PA 19380
Tel: (610) 431-4262

Philadelphia Mediation Group
Michael J. Bopp   F
191 Presidential Blvd Ste. 106
Bala Cynwyd, PA 19004
Tel: (610) 664-8209

Riegler, Elliot   F
2151 Linglestown Rd Ste. 200
Harrisburg, PA 17110
Tel: (717) 540-1313
Fax; (717) 540-1416

Rubin, Fredric David   F
2 Firewood Drive
Holland, PA 18966
Tel: (215) 860-2525
Fax: (215) 677-5131

Shopp, Judy   F
2935 Broxton Lane
York, PA 17402
Tel: (717) 755-4224
Fax: (717) 840-1455

Specialists in Divorce Mediation
Jerry M. Lazaroff   F
1029 N. Providence Road
Media, PA 19063
Tel: (610) 566-6633

Sutton, Richard D.   F
208 Stonybrook Drive
Norristown, PA 19403
Tel: (610) 768-2154
Fax: (610) 768-2470

Zitomer, Deborah   F
1600 Market Street Ste. 3600
Philadelphia, PA 19103
Tel: (215) 751-2141
Fax: (215) 751-2205

RHODE ISLAND

Bettigole, Bryna B.   F
29 Wilcox Avenue
Pawtucket, RI 02860
Tel: (401) 723-0353

Chernick, Debra L.   F
336 Main Street
Wakefield, RI 02879
Tel: (401) 789-1616
Fax: (401) 783-0660

Cosel, Peter   CA CM F
35 Long Wharf Mall
Newport, RI 02840
Tel: (401) 847-0970
Fax: (401) 847-0970

Dahl, Gloria   F
16 Maragansa Avenue
Jamestown, RI 02835
Tel: (401) 423-3700
Fax: (401) 423-2929

East Coast Med. Services   CA
R. D'Addario/J. Skinner   CM F
One Courthouse Square
Newport, RI 02840
Tel: (401) 849-0880
Fax: (401) 849-0897

Mediation Consultants   CM CA
J. M. Keating & K. Birt   F S N
50 South Main Street
Providence, RI 02903
Tel: (401) 274-5383
Fax: (401) 521-3555

Quigley, John L. Jr.   F
915 Smith Street
Providence, RI 02908
Tel: (401) 331-9090
Fax: (401) 521-7330

198

SOUTH CAROLINA

Bryan, Mary Lowndes   F
1528 Blanding Street
Columbia, SC 29201
Tel: (803) 252-5905
Fax: (803) 748-9220

Dispute Resolution Services Inc.
Nancy M. Young   F
P.O. Box 8626
Columbia, SC 29202
Tel: (803) 799-7666
Fax: (803) 252-3035

Family Mediation Services
Joyce Fields/F. Glenn Smith   F
2212 Devine Street
Columbia, SC 29205
Tel: (803) 799-2323
Fax: (803) 799-8249

Hamrick, Diane David   F
655 Street Andrews Blvd.
Charleston, SC 29407
Tel: (803) 571-2040
Fax: (803) 556-0701

Harness, Julie C.   F
11 49th Avenue
Isle of Palms, SC 29451
Tel: (803) 884-6473

Harness III, Cotton C.   F
117 Meeting Street
Charleston, SC 29402
Tel: (803) 853-1300
Fax: (803) 853-9992

Hobbs, Sandra   F
117 Cove Court
Columbia, SC 29212
Tel: (803) 274-4211

Knox-Whitney, Kathleen   F
132 Forest Fern Road
Columbia, SC 29208
Tel: (803) 777-5291
Fax: (803) 777-3498

Mediation Associates
Barbara Melton   F
171 Church St. Ste. 300
Charleston, SC 29401
Tel: (803) 723-8002
Fax: (803) 723-8002

Upchurch, Donna Wilson   F
1403 ½ Calhoun Street
Columbia, SC 29201
Tel: (803) 252-1866

SOUTH DAKOTA

Berget, J. Lee   F
P.O. Box 578
Sioux Falls, SD 57101
Tel: (605) 371-3017

Midwest Mediation
Tamara Trussell   CM
P.O. Box 1001
Sioux Falls, SD 57101-1001
Tel: (605) 339-1972
Fax: (605) 339-0082

TENNESSEE

Barker, Ann   F
8128 Chesterfield Drive
Knoxville, TN 37909
Tel: (615) 694-4571
Fax: (615) 694-9873

Barton, Lynn P.   F
4535 Harding Road #102
Nashville, TN 37205
Tel: (615) 269-4557

Davis, Gregory S.   F
4933 Wise Hills Road
Knoxville, TN 37920
Tel: (615) 579-1356
Fax: (615) 577-0561

McMahan, Katherine   F
415 Georgia Avenue
Chattanooga, TN 37403
Tel: (615) 756-4653
Fax: (615) 756-8120

Med. Services of Oak Ridge .
Margaret Devany Burns   F
1345 Oak Ridge Turnpike M350
Oak Ridge, TN 37830
Tel: (615) 481-3555

Peterson Mediation Institute
Mary Ann Zaha   F
7400 River Ridge Drive
Chattanooga, TN 37416-1092
Tel: (615) 877-3902

Redden, Jack   F
752 Crossover Lane
Memphis, TN 38117
Tel: (901) 682-3371
Fax: (901) 763-3272

Taylor, Virginia D.   F
7134 Highway 100
Nashville, TN 37221
Tel: (615) 356-5343

TEXAS

Abrams, Jeffery S.   CM F S
815 Hawthorne
Houston, TX 77006
Tel: (713) 527-0511

Adams, C. Kent   CA CM
2200 Ross Avenue Ste. 900
Dallas, TX 75201
Tel: (214) 220-4800
Fax: (214) 220-4899

Anderson, Michael R.   F
308 S. 3rd Street
Harlingen, TX 78550
Tel: (210) 425-8077
Fax: (210) 425-8077

Bean, Molly   F
2502 Barton Hills Drive
Austin, TX 78704
Tel: (512) 476-3323
Fax: (512) 476-0108

Bryant, Suzanne   F
1209 West 5th Street
Austin, TX 78703-5255
Tel: (512) 476-4760
Fax: (512) 476-4799

DiNoto, Caroline   F
17115 Red Oak Drive #109
Houston, TX 77090
Tel: (713) 893-4111
Fax: (713) 893-8082

Family & Business Mediation
Judy Kurth Dougherty   F
909 Kipling
Houston, TX 77006
Tel: (713) 521-9551
Fax: (713) 521-9828

Garber, Martha Ann   F
580 Denton Tap Road Ste. 270
Coppell, TX 75019
Tel: (214) 247-4902
Fax: (214) 304-0400

Greenstone, James L.   F
6211 W. Northwest Hwy Ste C
Dallas, TX 75225
Tel: (214) 361-0209
Fax: (214) 361-6545

Hack, Linda   F
P.O. Box 595314
Dallas, TX 75359
Tel: (214) 698-8307
Fax: (214) 761-1851

Hagen, William T.   F
16010 Barker Point Ste. 215
Houston, TX 77079
Tel: (713) 870-8020
Fax: (713) 870-0850

James, Paula   F
2905 San Gabriel Street #216
Austin, TX 78705
Tel: (512) 476-3400
Fax: (512) 469-9867

Kirkpatrick, Gary J.   F
2401 Turtle Creek Blvd.
Dallas, TX 75219
Tel: (800) 888-8609
Fax: (214) 328-9397

Leviton, Sharon   F
6211 W. Northwest High. #2806
Dallas, TX 75225
Tel: (214) 361-0209

Med. Associates of Houston CM
Carol. Hoffman /Jeanne Lee   F
Don Graul & Michael Hiller
4550 Post Oak Place Ste. 150
Houston, TX 77027
Tel: (713) 629-1416
Fax: (713) 629-1433

Slaikeu, Karl A.   F
1717 W. 6th St. #215
Austin, TX 78703
Tel: (512) 482-0356
Fax: (512) 474-4645

200

South Plains Dispute Resolution
D. Gene Valentini   F
P.O. Box 3730
Lubbock, TX 79452
Tel: (806) 762-8721
Fax: (806) 765-9544

The Mediation Group Inc.
Susanne C. Adams   F
2401 Turtle Creek Blvd.
Dallas, TX 75219
Tel: (214) 238-5050
Fax: (214) 238-1499

Twomey, Karen L.   F
1023 South Fleishel
Tyler, TX 75701
Tel: (903) 592-8374
Fax: (903) 592-5293

Yingling, Lynelle C.   F
570 E. Quail Run Road
Rockwall, TX 75087
Tel: (214) 771-9985
Fax: (214) 772-3669

UTAH
Accord Mediation
Marcella L. Keck   F
6914 South 3000 E #205
Salt Lake City, UT 84121
Tel: (801) 944-5400
Fax: (801) 944-8761

Albright, Dixie & William   F
2612 South 450 East
Bountiful, UT 84010
Tel: (801) 292-1269

Downes, William W.   F
175 W. 200 South Ste. 4000
Salt Lake City, UT 84101
Tel: (801) 322-2222
Fax: (801) 532-3706

VERMONT
A Mediation Partnership
Susan Feldman-Fay   F
P.O. Box 321
Fairfax, VT 05454
Tel: (800) 564-6859
Fax: (802) 849-6975

Bryan, Lee W.   F
475 Tansy Hill
Stowe, VT 05672
Tel: (802) 253-4113
Fax: (802) 253-9496

Conflict Resolution Associates
Ellen Bernstein   F
78 Central Avenue
South Burlington, VT 05403
Tel: (802) 658-2578

Estey, Alice   F
RFD 1, Box 65A
Vernon, VT 05354
Tel: (802) 257-5606
Fax: (802) 254-7725

Holistic Justice Center   CA CM
Bill van Zyverden   F S N
P.O. Box 753
Middlebury, VT 05753
Tel: (802) 388-7478

Hollyday, Ellen D.   F
P.O. Box 528
Windsor, VT 05089-0528
Tel: (802) 436-2964
Fax: (802) 436-2964

Kennedy, Marianne   F
RR 1, Box 2330
Arlington, VT 05250
Tel: (802) 375-9552
Fax: (802) 375-9552

Mediation Matters
Carl D. Schneider   F
Bear Hill Road RR 2, Box 191D
Randolph, VT 05060
Tel: (802) 276-3145
Fax: (802) 276-3004

Middlebury Mediation Center
Jennifer Barker   F
P.O. Box 735
Middlebury, VT 05753
Tel: (802) 388-3212

Swaim, Nina   F
Box 65
Sharon, VT 05065
Tel: (802) 763-2208
Fax: (802) 763-2238

Terry, Susanne   F
Road 2, Box 175
Johnsbury, VT 05819
Tel: (802) 748-3512
Fax: (802) 748-3512

Vermont Ctr for Conflict Res.
Lyn DuMoulin/David Desautels
76 St Paul St # 600   CA CM F S
Burlington, VT 05401
Tel: (802) 864-0902
Fax: (802) 864-8172

VIRGINIA
Alternative Dispute Resolution
Alexander C. Cullison   F
9341 Tovito Drive
Fairfax, VA 22031
Tel: (703) 691-0403
Fax: (703) 691-0403

Birdzell, Valerie   F
1504 Woodduck Road
Suffolk, VA 23433
Tel: (804) 363-8225

Cascades Mediation
Vincent Kavanagh   CM F
21495 Ridgetop Circle Ste. 304
Sterling, VA 20166
Tel: (703) 430-4600
Fax: (703) 430-5500

Common Ground Med. Svc.
Reggie Gordon   CM F
311 W. Franklin Street
Richmond, VA 23220
Tel: (804) 346-5700
Fax: (804) 780-1950

Community Mediation Center
Susan Hess   F
36 Southgate Court Ste, 102
Harrisonburg, VA 22801-9668
Tel: (703) 434-0059
Fax: (703) 434-0399

Community Mediation Center
Edwin C. Bumbaugh   F
36 Southgate Court, Ste. 102
Harrisonburg, VA 22801
Tel: (540) 434-0059
Fax: (540) 574-0174

Conflict Resolutions
Jerri Shevlin   F
12476 Sweet Leaf Terrace
Fairfax, VA 22033
Tel: (703) 385-3383

Dispute Alternatives
Joe Beaty   F
101 E. Main St.
Marion, VA 24354
Tel: (703) 783-7015
Fax: (703) 782-9474

Dispute Settlement Center
Judy S. Rubin   F
3608 Tidewater Center
Norfolk, VA 23509
Tel: (804) 625-9616
Fax: (804) 627-1394

Divorce Mediation Service
Jerome Bagnell   F
6104 Holly Arbor Court
Chester, VA 23831-7760
Tel: (804) 768-1000
Fax: (804) 768-1010

Fairfield, Kathryn Stolzfus   F
303 Nations Bank Bldg.
Harrisonburg, VA 22801
Tel: (540) 432-6144
Fax; (540) 532-0953

Family Med. Of Greater WA
Lawrence Gaughan   F
10300 Eaton Place #310
Fairfax, VA 22030-2239
Tel: (703) 273-4005
Fax: (703) 273-4006

Family Med. Svcs of Roanoke
Catherine M. Whittaker   F
3959 Electric Road
Roanoke, VA 24018
Tel: (540) 772-3108
Fax; (540) 774-6396

Family Med. of Northern VA
Jeffrey P. Sprowls   F
7918 Jones Branch Dr. Ste. 600
McLean, VA 22102
Tel: (703) 918-4950
Fax: (703) 918-4949

Foskett, Kathy F
6206 Sierra Court
Manassas, VA 22111
Tel: (703) 335-5827

Hartmann-Harlan, Martha F
915 Kingsland Road
Richmond, VA 23231
Tel: (804) 795-9283

Hubard, Tazewell T. III F
125 St. Paul's Blvd Ste. 201
Norfolk, VA 23510
Tel: (804) 627-6120
Fax: (804) 625-2161

Institute for Conflict Mngt.
Linda Hale F
3783 Center Way
Fairfax, VA 22033
Tel: (703) 591-3800
Fax: (703) 352-7714

Kavanagh, Vincent F. F
301 Linden Court
Sterling, VA 20164
Tel: (703) 437-4147

Key Bridge Therapy & Med.
Emily M. Brown F
1925 N. Lynn Street Ste. 700
Arlington, VA 22209
Tel: (703) 528-3900
Fax: (703) 524-5666

Lohman, Mark R. F
1 Village Green Circle
Charlottesville, VA 22905
Tel: (703) 442-9090
Fax: (804) 977-2944

Massey, A. Blanton F
1119 Caroline Street
Frederickburg, VA 22404-0240
Tel: (703) 373-1818
Fax: (703) 373-5306

Mast, Ervin J. F
8470 Brunger St.
Manassa, VA 22111
Tel: (703) 941-9008
Fax: (703) 750-0621

Med. Consultants of Tidewater
Karen Asaro F
1117 Ewell Road
Virginia Beach, VA 23455
Tel: (804) 363-8225

Mediation Center
Lucy Lutterbie F
P.O. Box 1944
Frederickburg, VA 22402
Tel: (703) 373-0549

Mediation Services of Virginia
William J. Shepherd F
1861 Rosemont Lane
Hayes, VA 23072
Tel: (804) 642-5141

Moore, Catherine L. F
P.O. Box 7107
Richmond, VA 23221-0107
Tel: (804) 355-5944
Fax: (804) 355-9922

Myricks,Noel F
2000 Golf Course Drive
Reston, VA 22091
Tel: (301) 405-4007
Fax: (703) 716-0193

Northern Virginia Mediation
Harriet Koplan F
4103 Chain Bridge Road
Fairfax, VA 22032
Tel: (703) 993-3656
Fax: (703) 934-5142

Peninsula Mediation Center
D. Samuelson & M. Eckles F
P.O. Box 7135
Hampton, VA 23666
Tel: (804) 838-0148
Fax: (804) 357-3481

West, Dennis Micha F
6356 Meeting House Way
Alexandria, VA 22312
Tel: (703) 256-2871

Whittaker Mediation Associates
Robert L. Whitaker F
8716 Ruggles Road
Richmond, VA 23229
Tel: (804) 288-0796
Fax: (804) 648-3115

Zelinger-Casway, Robin   F
9401 Courthouse Road #201
Chesterfield, VA 23832
Tel: (804) 748-3250

WASHINGTON

Amicus Dispute Resolution
Jayne Bauer-Hughes   F
P.O. Box 337
South Bend, WA 98586
Tel: (800) 231-3422
Fax: (360) 875-5290

Bergquist, A. Bruce   F
203 4th Avenue E. #320
Olympia, WA 98501
Tel: (360) 705-1512
Fax: (360) 956-1277

Clelland, Ted, Jr.   CA CM
600 University Street Ste. 2000
Seattle, WA 98101
Tel: (206) 467-0793
Fax: (206) 467-7810

Cockrill, Patrick R.   F
P.O. Box 487
Yakima, WA 98907
Tel: (509) 575-1500
Fax: (509) 575-1227

Conflict Management
Larry Rogers   CA CM N
P.O. Box 12240
Olympia, WA 98508-2240
Tel: (360) 866-8920

Conflict Resolution Unlimited
Nancy Kaplan   F
845 106th Ave., NE Ste. 109
Bellevue, WA 98004
Tel: (206) 451-4015
Fax: (206) 451-1477

Eberle Mediation Services
Richard M. Eberle   F
10900 NE 8th Street #900
Bellevue, WA 98004
Tel: (206) 454-0724
Fax: (206) 450-9864

Family Mediation Services
Barbara A. Rofkar   F
1155 North State Street #524
Bellingham, WA 98225
Tel: (206) 671-6416

Hatzenbeler, Mary J.   F
316 E. 4th Plain Blvd.
Vancouver, WA 98663
Tel: (360) 695-6188
Fax: (360) 737-7686

Jeffers, Judith   F
1721 Evergreen Place
Seattle, WA 98122
Tel: (206) 325-4242
Fax: (206) 325-4242

Northwest Mediation Associates
Samuel Mahaffy   CM F
107 S. Howard, Ste. 419
Spokane, WA 99204
Tel: (509) 459-1734
Fax: (509) 327-9866

Pacific Family Med. Institute
Susan Dearborn   F
12505 Bel-Red Road #211
Bellevue, WA 98005
Tel: (206) 451-7940
Fax: (206)324-4945

Schweinfurth, Ruth   F
844 Fern Court
Walla Walla, WA 99362
Tel: (509) 525-2539

Smith, Pamela   F
18611 68th St. East
Bonny Lake, WA 98390
Tel: (206) 863-9653

Stipe, Sue A.   F
33919 9th Avenue South #201
Federal Way, WA 98003
Tel: (206) 467-1722 EXT 1489

Symons, Mary   F
Star Route, Box 95
Olga, WA 98279
Tel: (206) 376-4549
Fax: (206) 376-2626

Watson, Lars S.   F
3421 NW 64th Street
Seattle, WA 98107
Tel: (206) 784-0919

Wilburn, Donnelly J.   F
2815 130th Place NE
Bellevue, WA 98005
Tel: (206) 453-8452
Fax: (206) 637-9541

WEST VIRGINIA
Amores, Constantino CA CM F
901 Quarrier Street Ste. 206
Charleston, WV 25301
Tel: (304) 343-1692
Fax: (304) 343-5830

WISCONSIN
Ackerman, Marc J.   F
250 West Coventry Crt. Ste. 209
Milwaukee, WI 53217
Tel: (414) 351-0066
Fax: (414) 351-6772

Bellman, Howard   CA CM N
123 E. Main St
Madison, WI 53703
Tel: (608) 255-9393
Fax: (608) 255-9593

Costrini-Norgal, Rita   F
51 South Main Street
Janesville, WI 53545
Tel: (608) 757-5549

Fullin, James   CM S N
123 E. Main Street
Madison, WI 53703-3315
Tel: (800) 397-9909
Fax: (608) 250-6395

Greenlee, Rebecca E.   F
P.O. Box 5086
Madison, WI 53705
Tel: (608) 238-7122
Fax: (608) 238-9606

Hampton, Marilyn   F
3002 Begonia Street
Wausau WI 54401
Tel: (715) 847-5723

Kahn, Lawrence   CA CM F
8989 N Port Wash. Rd Ste. 207
Bayside, WI 53217
Tel: (414) 351-1945
Fax: (414) 352-6577

Mediation Center
John & Stephanie Hamann   F
710 North Main Box 405
River Falls, WI 54022
Tel: (715) 425-9558
Fax: (715) 425-1055

New Prospects
Susan Bronson   CM F
1219 N. Cass Street
Milwaukee, WI 53202
Tel: (414) 291-9487

Out of Court Solutions CA FCM
Thomas Dulde/Sandra Scherer
Margaret Miota/Robert Schuelke
3033 S. 128th Street
New Berlin, WI 53151
Tel: (414) 821-9462
Fax: (414) 821-9461

Pilati, David   CM F S N
4154 N. Lake Drive
Milwaukee, WI 53211
Tel: (414) 962-2777
Fax: (414) 963-2135

Wylie, John G.   F
331 E. Washington Street
Appleton, WI 54911
Tel: (414) 739-2366
Fax: (414) 739-8893

WYOMING
Balis Park Co. Family Mediation
Elizabeth Goodyear   F
1323 Sunset Blvd #2048
Cody, WY 82414
Tel: (307) 527-5239
Fax; (307) 527-5301

Jett, Juliet & Tolman, Anton   F
75 Yellow Creek Road Ste. 305
Evanston, WY 82930
Tel: (307) 789-6773
Fax: (307) 789-3244

MEDIATION TRAINING WORKSHOPS

Allen and Mohr present mediation training workshops throughout the United States, and in other countries by invitation. To request information about these workshops, call 800-748-6462 or send your request via E-mail to:Staff @ctcmediation.com.

ORDER FORM

* Fax: 619-436-7943 (fax this form)
☎ Telephone: 800-494-9866 (have information on form ready)
❏ Internet: Westcoastpress@ctcmediation.com
✉ Regular Mail: West Coast Press, 4401 Manchester Ave., Ste. 202, Encinitas, CA 92024

Please send_____copies of **Affordable Justice**.
Company name_____
Name_____
Address_____
City_____State_____Zip_____
Telephone_____
Fax_____
E-Mail_____

Price: $19.95

Sales tax: Please add 7.75% ($1.55 per book) for books shipped to California addresses.

Shipping: by First Class Mail in the U.S.: $3.00. Call for amounts for other countries.

Payment amount: Book(s)........ $ _____
Tax.............. $ _____
Shipping...... $ _____
Total........... $ _____

Check_____Visa/MasterCard_____Exp. Date_____
Acct.#_____
Name on Acct._____